UNDERSTANDING CRIME AND SOCIAL POLICY

Also available in the series

Understanding research for social policy and social work (second edition)
Themes, methods and approaches
Edited by Saul Becker, Alan Bryman and Harry Ferguson

"Takes you on a fascinating journey through the world of social research and is so well written it is a joy to read ... a superb text ... an outstanding organizational and intellectual achievement." *International Journal of Social Research Methodology*

"Becker and Bryman did a masterful job...North American public policy students could learn a lot from this book and methodology instructors could have their load considerably eased if URfSPP was more widely read." Kennedy Stewart, Associate Professor, Simon Fraser University School of Public Policy and Member of Parliament for Burnaby-Douglas (review of first edition)

PB £24.99 (US$42.95) **ISBN** 978 1 84742 815 8 **HB** £65.00 (US$89.95) **ISBN** 978 1 84742 816 5
448 pages March 2012
INSPECTION COPY AVAILABLE

Understanding health and social care (second edition)
Themes, methods and approaches
Jon Glasby

"This is an ambitious and wide-ranging book which provides a valuable historical perspective, as well as a forward-looking analysis, based on real experience. It will be a valuable tool for leaders, policy makers and students." Nigel Edwards, Policy Director, The NHS Confederation

PB £21.99 (US$34.95) **ISBN** 978 1 84742 623 9 **HB** £65.00 (US$85.00) **ISBN** 978 1 84742 624 6
224 pages February 2012
INSPECTION COPY AVAILABLE

Understanding 'race' and ethnicity
Theory, history, policy, practice
Gary Craig, Karl Atkin, Sangeeta Chattoo and Ronny Flynn

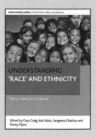

"The title of this text belies the far-reaching challenge it poses to the discipline, research base and practice of social policy. Its argument that mainstream social policy has consistently marginalised the issue of 'race' and minority ethnic concerns is well founded when judged against the historical record, the evidence base and contemporary shortfalls in policy and practice. This is a deep exploration of the complexities of diversity and difference that speaks to contemporary concerns about substantive citizenship and social justice." Professor Charlotte Williams, OBE, Keele University.

PB £22.99 (US$38.95) **ISBN** 978 1 84742 770 0 **HB** £65.00 (US$85.00) **ISBN** 978 1 84742 771 7
336 pages February 2012
INSPECTION COPY AVAILABLE

For a full listing of all titles in the series visit www.policypress.co.uk

www.policypress.co.uk

INSPECTION COPIES AND ORDERS AVAILABLE FROM:
Marston Book Services • PO BOX 269 • Abingdon • Oxon OX14 4YN UK
INSPECTION COPIES
Tel: +44 (0) 1235 465500 • Fax: +44 (0) 1235 465556 • Email: inspections@marston.co.uk
ORDERS
Tel: +44 (0) 1235 465500 • Fax: +44 (0) 1235 465556 • Email: direct.orders@marston.co.uk

UNDERSTANDING CRIME AND SOCIAL POLICY

Emma Wincup

First published in Great Britain in 2013 by
Policy Press
University of Bristol
Fourth Floor, Beacon House
Queen's Road
Bristol BS8 1QU
UK
t: +44 (0)117 331 4054
f: +44 (0)117 331 4093
tpp-info@bristol.ac.uk
www.policypress.co.uk

North American office:
Policy Press
c/o The University of Chicago Press
1427 East 60th Street
Chicago, IL 60637, USA
t: +1 773 702 7700
f: +1 773 702 9756
sales@press.uchicago.edu
www.press.uchicago.edu

© Policy Press and the Social Policy Association 2013

British Library Cataloguing in Publication Data
A catalogue record for this book is available from the British Library.

Library of Congress Cataloging-in-Publication Data
A catalog record for this book has been requested.

ISBN 978 1 84742 499 0 paperback
ISBN 978 1 84742 500 3 hardcover

The right of Emma Wincup to be identified as author of this work has been asserted by her in accordance with the Copyright, Designs and Patents Act 1988.

The statements and opinions contained within this publication are solely those of the author and not of the University of Bristol, Policy Press or the Social Policy Association. The University of Bristol, Policy Press and the Social Policy Association disclaim responsibility for any injury to persons or property resulting from any material published in this publication.

Policy Press works to counter discrimination on grounds of gender, race, disability, age and sexuality.

Cover design by Qube Design Associates, Bristol.
Front cover: photograph kindly supplied by www.alamy.com
Printed and bound in Great Britain by Hobbs, Southampton.
Policy Press uses environmentally responsible print partners.

Contents

Detailed contents

List of boxes and tables

Boxes

Tables

Preface and acknowledgements

Understanding crime and social policy has had a long gestation period. Initial discussions took place before becoming a parent, for the second time, to a daughter who, in a few months, will be heading off to school. This is a very real reminder of how much of a debt I owe to Ali Shaw at The Policy Press for her tremendous patience when, like many academics, I struggled to fit writing into an increasingly hectic schedule. Without her support I would have given up a long time ago. I'd also like to thank the anonymous reviewer for the encouragement to continue when I was so close and yet so far, and Jo Morton for her attention to detail as the manuscript was transformed into the finished book.

Writing the book has taken me back to aspects of my own academic studies, which had been long forgotten. Researching Chapter Three allowed me to dust off my political science books and reminded me of the value of an interdisciplinary engagement, which this book aims to encourage. At the University of Leeds I have been fortunate enough to teach social policy (although I haven't always called it that) to undergraduate and postgraduate criminology and criminal justice students, as well as those who have been tempted across from law and subjects far less closely related. Much of the material contained within the book has already been tried out in different forms in *Crime and social exclusion* and *Criminal justice policies, perspectives and research*. I'd particularly like to thank the postgraduate classes of 2011 for the lively discussions.

As well as being shaped by my experiences of teaching, *Understanding crime and social policy* also draws on research projects and publications I have worked on with Anthea Hucklesby, Stuart Lister and, more recently, with Mark Monaghan. In particular, the many conversations I have had with Anthea in various teashops while waiting to be let back into prison after lunch have influenced Chapter Five. The book also benefits enormously (I hope!) from my role as editor of the *Journal of Social Policy* between 2004 and 2008. I am very grateful to Jan Pahl for inviting me to edit the journal, broadening my understanding of social policy and introducing me to the social policy 'community'.

This book is dedicated to Ben and Amelia. They will be thrilled at seeing their names in print, and now that it is complete, I promise to rectify the 'parenting deficit' that one day they might read about in Chapter Seven.

one

Introducing crime and social policy

In August 2011, for several nights in cities across the UK a significant number of members of the public became involved in civil unrest. Beginning initially in Tottenham in London, the disturbances quickly spread to a number of other London boroughs and further afield, mostly to major cities such as Birmingham, Liverpool and Manchester. Media coverage was constant, depicting images of violent protest, seemingly mindless vandalism and rampant looting, which the police struggled to contain. Iconic images such as a woman jumping from her flat in a burning building in London into the arms of rescuers captured the dramatic nature of the events. Afterwards images of criminal acts were replaced by those of destroyed city centres and lost livelihoods, and were accompanied by reports of courts sitting through the night to issue harsh sentences to punish those deemed responsible at the earliest possible opportunity. The removal of welfare benefits from convicted rioters was also suggested by Iain Duncan Smith (Work and Pensions Secretary), which received some, but not full, support from members of the Coalition government. Inevitably there have been numerous different interpretations of the urban disturbances, ranging from the then Justice Secretary Ken Clarke's view that they represented 'sheer casual criminality' (quoted in Hope, 2011), predominantly by a 'feral underclass' (Clarke, 2011), through to more nuanced accounts which locate such behaviour in its socioeconomic contexts. Research by the London School of Economics and Political Science and *The Guardian* (Lewis et al, 2011) found that the rioters frequently identified political grievances, justifying their behaviour with reference to broader policy developments that they felt were unjust, such as cuts in public spending. Social policy cannot be blamed for the riots, nor does social policy offer all the solutions to preventing such acts happening again. However, this example encourages reflection on the many connections between crime and social policy. This book contributes in a small way to what is certainly a more ambitious project.

Crime and criminal justice policy has only rarely been a key concern of social policy academics. Social policy journals contain relatively few articles on crime, and social policy conferences attract only a handful of papers on crime and its control. Instead, understanding crime and how best to control it has been left largely to criminologists, who have frequently investigated the relationship between social problems and crime, but often without serious engagement with ongoing social policy debates about the same issues. There has also been little attempt to reflect on the connections between the two disciplines (Rodger, 2008b), although there are notable exceptions (see, for example, Knepper, 2007). To understand why, it is helpful to consider how social policy is typically defined. As Bochel and Bochel (2004) note, academic social policy has frequently been characterised by the major policy areas it has concerned itself with including, for example, health, education and social security. Typically, it has been preoccupied with welfare provision, but as it has expanded to include new areas, for example, environmental policy (see, for example, Fitzpatrick, 2011), it becomes difficult to define it in this way. While one response might be to open up a debate about whether these new areas can actually be characterised as social policy, imposing somewhat arbitrary disciplinary boundaries is not helpful. More fluid definitions of social policy offer considerable advantages. Dean (2006: 1) describes social policy as 'the study of human wellbeing'. Defined in these terms, crime becomes a key concern for social policy academics in the same way that crime is already a concern for social policy professionals who work in fields such as housing, public health and social services. Increasingly these individuals work alongside criminal justice professionals in multi-agency teams to promote community safety, address drug use and respond to youth crime (see Chapters Four to Seven). Linking criminology and social policy has the potential to advance common theoretical understanding of trends across a diverse range of policy areas. Within both disciplines, the criminalisation of social policy has been recognised, with commentators noting how the traditional goals of social policy have increasingly been supplemented, and possibly replaced, with the desire to control crime in areas such as housing and education policy (see Chapter Two). For criminologists, the focus has typically been on the growing pre-occupation with controlling anti-social behaviour (for more recent examples, see Burney, 2009; Donoghue, 2010), while social policy academics have been concerned with New Labour's social exclusion agenda (see Rodger, 2008b). These are connected by a desire to discipline those who do not engage in behaviours expected of the responsible citizen, which increasingly relate to engagement in the labour market. The case studies in Chapters Six and Seven elucidate what is often referred to as the 'politics of behaviour' and the connections between welfare and discipline.

At first glance the inclusion of a book on crime in a series entitled 'Understanding Welfare' appears as an awkward anomaly. Crime policy abandoned its commitment to penal welfarism in the late 1970s when rising crime rates, despite improved social conditions, led to the now infamous claims that 'nothing works' (for a more detailed historical overview, see Raynor and Robinson, 2009). The dominant justification for punishment at the time – rehabilitation – was largely abandoned in favour of a new culture of control, with its emphasis on populist punitiveness and public protection, alongside the 'commodification' of crime control (Christie, 2000; Garland, 2001). However, as we discuss throughout this book, the welfare state has increasingly become part of the state apparatus to manage crime and anti-social behaviour, playing multiple roles including promoting compliance with community sentences, regulating the behaviour of those who have engaged in criminal or anti-social acts and addressing the root causes of crime. Welfare reform became a key part of New Labour's crime reduction agenda, and this has evolved under the Conservative–Liberal Democrat Coalition, lending support for the argument that a new 'welfare settlement' has emerged. Thus, even if welfare is defined somewhat narrowly as the provision of support to those in need, it appears that crime should be central to understanding welfare. Adopting a broader definition of welfare focused on human wellbeing, there is no need to question the inclusion of a book on crime in the series: crime and fear of it shapes the lives of many, causing the greatest harm to some of the poorest and most excluded members of society (Pantazis, 2000, 2006).

Understanding crime and social policy seeks to explore further the interface between crime and social policy, drawing on theoretical developments and empirical research from within both criminology and social policy. Focusing on the policy process, it explores the multiplicity of influences that shape the formulation and delivery of crime control policies. Policy in this context has multiple meanings, and as Bochel and Bochel (2004) imply, it is more useful to reflect on the different ways the term is deployed than to attempt to select from the multiple definitions available. Following this advice, the term 'policy' is used in this book to refer to a field of activity (for example, penal policy or drug policy), the positions adopted by organisations such as political parties, think tanks and pressure groups (see Chapter Three), government programmes (for example, the Crime Reduction Programme described in Chapter Three, **Box 3.3**), as well as more specific proposals, sometimes originating from legislation. While exploring the policy process relating to crime and its control, connections will be made to wider social, economic and political agendas that influence social policy more broadly.

Understanding crime and social policy is written principally with two audiences in mind. The first is students across the disciplines of criminology and social policy. The second is employees from the public, private and voluntary sector undertaking professional training relating to crime. Being mindful of these two audiences has shaped the nature of the book. One of its key aims is to encourage readers to engage further with the issues and debates through discussing the questions that accompany each chapter, following up the suggested readings and browsing the recommended websites.

Given the increasing interconnections between crime and social policy, it follows that a book of only 164 pages will inevitably be partial. With this in mind it is useful to set some parameters. First, the book concentrates on the period between 1979 and 2012. The rapidly changing policy landscape presents a challenge for readers, who are encouraged to use the websites identified at the end of this chapter to keep abreast of policy developments and debates surrounding them. The start date is the beginning of the first Thatcher government. There is, of course, a danger of attaching too much significance to particular dates and over-emphasising the degree of change produced by a new government. However, in this instance the choice of date can be defended – Thatcher uniquely gave her name to refer to a distinctive form of politics. With respect to crime policy, her legacy was to argue for a strong authoritarian state to take responsibility for controlling crime but to allow others, principally the private sector, to become involved in the actual delivery of criminal justice (Farrall and Hay, 2010; Hough, 2011). At the same time, it is worth noting that the Thatcher governments (1979–90) produced less radical changes to crime policy than many other social policy areas. Indeed, as Farrall and Hay (2010) note, Thatcherite ideas did not have an impact on crime policy initially, and the main effects were only witnessed after she had left office. Moreover, the literature on the politics of crime controls identifies 1979 as a watershed year when charting the increased politicisation of law and order (for an introductory overview, see Hale and Fitzgerald, 2009). Downes and Morgan (2012) propound that law and order only became part of contested party politics in the mid-1960s, coming to the fore in 1979. Prior to that the main political parties were preoccupied with the project of reconstruction after the Second World War (1939–45) and there was an underlying consensus on the issue that dominates general election campaigns today. Rising crime rates – which the Conservatives blamed on previous Labour governments – led to the implicit bipartisan consensus on law and order issues breaking down. In essence the Conservatives used crime as a 'trump card' to undermine

Labour's ability to maintain order during a period of intense political protest and industrial dispute.

Second, the book focuses predominantly on UK policy, and more specifically on England and Wales. Other parts of the UK have their own criminal justice systems (see Croall et al, 2010, on Scotland, and Ellison and O'Mahoney, 2010, on Northern Ireland). Unlike other devolved parts of the UK, Wales does not have responsibility for many aspects of crime control: these fall under the remit of the Home Office and the Ministry of Justice. However, the Welsh Government does have responsibilities in relation to community safety, prioritising, among others, substance misuse, youth crime and domestic violence in its current *Programme for government* (Welsh Government, 2011).

Having introduced the parameters for the discussion that follows, we now turn our attention to the core concept – crime – and deconstructing what appears at first glance to be a common-sense category (see Morrison, 2009).

What is crime?

In late-modern society, crime is all-pervasive, not in the sense that we all frequently experience it (thankfully for most people this is a rare occurrence), but in the sense that we are pre-occupied with crime. For instance, representations of crime – particularly violent crime – feature heavily in our media diet, acting as 'a major source of concern ... distraction, resistance, escapism and moral reassurance' (Greer, 2009: 197). Given our current pre-occupation with 'crime', it is easy to lose sight of the fact that many of the acts that we now regard as criminal were previously defined in terms of 'sin', 'civil wrongs' or 'private disputes' (Muncie, 2001a). 'Modern' thinking on crime developed rapidly over the first two thirds of the 19th century, and during this period the criminal justice 'system' developed, leading to the emergence of a professional police force and a national prison system (Sharpe, 2001). Historical accounts of this period are numerous (for an accessible introduction, see Shore, 2009). Many draw attention to the ways in which crime became defined as a social problem, with concerns about crime reflecting broader anxieties about threats to social order, especially from the 'dangerous' classes; issues we return to in Chapter Two.

There is now an extensive literature that highlights the contested nature of crime (see, for example, Zedner, 2004; Morrison, 2009). Typically, discussions begin by challenging the notion that crime can be defined objectively with reference to the criminal law. Legal definitions are attractive because they appear to make it possible to identify criminal acts in a precise and unambiguous way, but the unproblematic nature of legal definitions is shattered on closer analysis. Even those acts on which we might expect consensus – the act of deliberately killing someone – proves to be controversial under certain circumstances – for example, if the 'victim' was terminally ill and requested that someone should help them to end their life. In this respect, criminologists have drawn attention to the social construction of criminal law, questioning the objective nature of the processes of law creation and enforcement. They note that acts that are criminalised are the outcome of a complex sequence of events, and to understand them we need to ask questions about norms and values, alongside posing questions relating to power and inequality. In essence, understanding crime requires an analysis of the nature of society as a whole, leading criminologists over the past four decades to reflect critically on whether society is characterised by consensus or whether it is more appropriate to recognise the different, sometimes competing, interests at work when acts are criminalised. Such an analysis offers space to question whether the criminal law reflects a shared understanding of what type of behaviours constitute the most harmful acts, or whether it represents the interests of only a proportion of society. Taking this analysis further, some criminologists have drawn attention to inequality in society, and argued that the criminal law serves to protect the interests of the most powerful groups. Noting the political nature of crime, critical criminologists have argued that there has been a tendency to criminalise acts of the powerless, while glossing over the arguably more harmful acts committed by powerful groups within society (DeKeseredy, 2011). Collectively, this process serves to protect the status quo, maintaining divisions based on class, 'race' and gender, among others. In response to this, some criminologists have argued that the concept of social harm is more theoretically coherent and politically progressive than the concept of crime (Hillyard and Tombs, 2008). This could encompass physical, financial/economic, emotional and psychological, and sexual harm, and recognise that behaviours that are not currently infringements of criminal law can have far-reaching effects. Examples include medical negligence, mis-selling of financial 'products' and discriminatory criminal justice practices.

Setting aside debates about legal definitions of crime, criminologists have also drawn attention to the ways in which criminal acts might be considered as violations of moral codes. Again a recurring theme in the literature is to reflect on whose morals become the dominant ones (and thus reflected in criminal law) for distinguishing between 'deviant' and 'normal' behaviour, and the lack of clear and unambiguous rules of what constitutes (un)acceptable behaviour is noted. If morality is used as a means of defining crime, potentially a wide range of behaviours could be conceptualised as 'wrongdoing'. This provides an opportunity to explore behaviours that are not defined as infringements of the criminal law. Yet at the same time it facilitates state intervention to contain behaviours that are not illegal but that are perceived to threaten the safety of communities. As we discuss in Chapter Two, New Labour's 'tough on crime' agenda had clear moral overtones in the way it focused on the disorderly, anti-social and nuisance behaviours of the new 'dangerous' classes. This agenda served to blur the boundaries between criminal and quasi (or sub-criminal) acts. In Cohen's (1979) terms, this agenda involves 'net widening', increasing the number of individuals, and particularly young people, subject to formal social control (see Brown, 2004). From a critical criminological perspective, it focused attention once more on the behaviour of the powerless, serving to regulate their behaviour not only through the usual mechanisms of crime control but also through social policy interventions.

Structure of the book

The remainder of the book is divided into seven chapters. **Chapter Two** elaborates further on many of the themes readers have been introduced to within this chapter, and looks at the trend towards increasing criminalisation. It focuses especially on the growing tendency to redefine social problems in terms of crime, anti-social behaviour and disorder, drawing attention to the interconnections between crime control and social policy, commonly described as the criminalisation of social policy. The next two chapters are dedicated to the crime policy process, exploring its development and implementation respectively. **Chapter Three** explores the range of competing influences on crime policy, including political influences (in every sense of the term), the public, media and researchers. In so doing, it challenges traditional conceptualisations of the policy process. In **Chapter Four** the range of players involved in delivering crime policies are explored. In addition to the 'usual suspects' working in the core criminal justice agencies, crime control increasingly involves individuals working in a wider range of public sector agencies plus private and voluntary sector organisations. **Chapters Five**, **Six** and **Seven** are case studies of three policy areas: the resettlement of prisoners, tackling problem drug use and working with 'troubled' families. These demonstrate the close connections, and sometimes tensions, between crime reduction and social policy. The choice of topics reflect issues which were high on New Labour's policy agenda, and which have continued to be salient ones for the Conservative–Liberal Democrat Coalition government. I should also confess that the first two reflect my own research interests, and as such they draw on empirical research studies conducted during the past decade. In particular, the case studies relate to three evaluations of resettlement projects (see Wincup and

Hucklesby, 2007), and ongoing policy analysis (since 2009) of the use of welfare reform as a strategy of crime and drug control. **Chapter Eight**, the concluding chapter, explores recurring themes within the book, which centre around the desire of neoliberal states to regulate behaviour using crime as a strategy of governance.

Guide to electronic resources

- *The Guardian* (www.guardian.co.uk/uk/ukcrime): *The Guardian*'s collection of its own news stories and articles on crime.
- **Home Office** (www.homeoffice.gov.uk): the Home Office is the lead government department for immigration and passports, drugs policy, crime, counter-terrorism and policing.
- The **Justice** website (www.justice.gov.uk): brings together the previously separate websites of government departments and national organisations concerned with justice including the Ministry of Justice, HM Prison Service and the National Offender Management Service.
- **Welsh Government** (http://wales.gov.uk/about/): under 'programme for government' you will find information about the community safety agenda that falls within the remit of the devolved Government of Wales.

two

Crime, criminalisation and social policy

Overview

In Chapter One we explored the contested nature of the concept of crime and drew attention to the increasingly blurred boundaries between crime and related concepts, namely, anti-social behaviour and disorder. This chapter looks at the trend towards increasing criminalisation, a process driven in part by the growing tendency to redefine social problems as threats to law and order. Widely referred to as the 'criminalisation of social policy', this process of redefinition is used to justify the imposition of either criminal or civil sanctions (but backed up by the threat of criminal sanctions for non-compliance) in some circumstances while serving, in a more general sense, to regulate the behaviour of large segments of the general public, such as parents of school-aged children or residents in social housing.

Key concepts
Anti-social behaviour, crime, criminalisation, dangerous classes, (dis)order, social problems

A recent history of criminalisation

Looking back at the past two centuries it is possible to identify numerous examples of acts being criminalised which traditionally were not interpreted as problems of crime. Notable examples include domestic violence (Saraga, 2001) and drug use (see Chapter Six). There is, of course, movement in the other direction with the legalisation of acts that had previously been defined as 'criminal'. An obvious example in this respect is the legalisation of homosexual acts for consenting men (initially only for those aged over 21) in the Sexual Offences Act 1967 (West and Woelke, 1997). On balance, it is fair to conclude that the number of criminal acts that have been legalised is far exceeded by the creation of new criminal offences.

Over the past 15 years, and particularly under the New Labour governments, there has been a rapid increase in the number of criminal offences on the statute books. While the exact number of new offences created is not known (see Morgan, 2012), Morgan (2011) argues that it is indisputable that there has been a huge increase in the number of incidents that the police and Crown Prosecution Service (CPS) can define as crime. In 2008 it was estimated that between 1997 and 2008, 3,605 offences were created, an average of 320 a year and almost one for every day in office (Morris, 2008). Of these just over one third (34 per cent) were introduced through primary legislation following parliamentary debates, with the remaining acts being criminalised through the use of secondary legislation, which involves the state using powers already conferred in primary legislation (for more detailed discussion on change to the law-making process, see Elliot and Quinn, 2011). By 2009 the number had increased to 4,289, indicating that the rate of introducing new offences had increased under the leadership of Gordon Brown (Collins, 2010). Newspapers – tabloids and broadsheets alike – were quick to condemn many of these crimes as frivolous and/or unnecessary (see Collins, 2010; Slack 2010). Similarly, the Liberal Democrats were also highly critical of what Chris Huhne – as their Home Office spokesperson – referred to as an 'acute and prolonged bout of legislative diarrhoea' (quoted in Collins, 2010). While such views may have considerable support, it is important not to gloss over the offences that were created during this period to respond to acts that almost all would perceive as harmful. For example, among the long list of offences created by New Labour are four racially aggravated offences (assaults, criminal damage, public order and harassment) introduced in the Crime and Disorder Act 1998 (see Rowe, 2012). In essence, criminalisation is not in itself wrong but, as we explore in this chapter, it can have unintended consequences, so such powers should be used judiciously.

The driving forces underpinning the project of increasing criminalisation are contested and, in some respects, controversial. They relate to different understandings of crime and the role of criminal law, which we explored in the first chapter. The most straightforward – and some may argue simplistic – explanation is that it is simply the government taking action against destructive acts. Governments are constantly subject to calls for criminalisation to address behaviours judged, at least by some sections of the public, to be problematic. It is therefore understandable that they will respond accordingly given the importance of garnering public support on law and order issues for electoral success. Many of the behaviours that were criminalised by New Labour were low-level acts that as ad hoc events can appear trivial but when they are experienced on an ongoing basis can have a detrimental impact on an individual's (or a community's) quality of life. For example, many people would be able to tolerate occasional noise from a neighbour's house when they host a party, but would find it difficult to cope with loud music on a daily basis in the early hours of the morning when they are trying to sleep. Consequently, measures to tackle these anti-social and/or disorderly behaviours, which we discuss shortly, often have popular support.

As we discuss in the next chapter, the public now plays a key role in the development of law and order policies. From this perspective the range of measures introduced can be justified as part of a wider project of 'rebalancing' the criminal justice system from the 'offender' towards the 'victim'. Such measures can also be defended on the grounds that they help to close the 'justice gap'. In the first instance, this referred to the problem of attrition within the criminal justice system: 'the gap between levels of known crime and the response of the criminal justice system in terms of prosecutions, convictions and sentencing' (Garside, 2004: 7). The 'victim' was used as a rhetorical and symbolic device to introduce crime control policies that can disadvantage those accused of crimes (Walklate, 2012), while having far wider implications. New Labour took on the ambitious project of creating quasi-offences that would be subject to criminal sanctions. Defined in these terms, the project of 'closing the justice gap' became synonymous with net widening, drawing more children, young people and adults into the criminal justice system through using formal sanctions to respond to marginally criminal behaviour which would have in the past resulted in more informal responses (Morgan, 2011).

Redefining social problems as 'crime'

As we explored in the introductory chapter, resorting to criminalisation in response to anxieties about the changing nature of society is not new. As Gatrell (1990: 386) argued with reference to the early 19th century,

> [C]rime was becoming a vehicle for articulating mounting anxieties about issues which really had nothing to do with crime at all: social change and the stability of the social hierarchy. These issues invested crime with new meanings, justified vastly accelerated action against it, and have determined attitudes to it ever since.

In a useful chapter that notes long-term continuities in societal responses to crime and criminals, Sharpe (2001) notes that the 'problem of crime' was constituted in the early 19th century as pathological acts committed by the 'criminal' or 'dangerous' classes, and the 'delinquent' behaviour of young people was a particular concern (see Pearson, 1983). The limited space available here precludes analysis of the complex origins of this development (see Wiener, 1990), but it is important to acknowledge the impact of the emerging middle class on policy-making (see Sharpe, 2001) and penal philanthropy (Garland, 1985). During the 19th century state intervention in crime control expanded rapidly. Like the development of criminology itself, it formed part of a 'modernist' project to 'solve' the 'problem of crime'. Modernity in this context refers to the belief that society is open to transformation through human intervention. To illustrate, in this period, a separate youth justice system emerged, not only to protect young people from being corrupted by older, more entrenched offenders, but also because it was felt that young people could be reformed (Kirton, 2009). The extent to which these, and other, developments, such as the growth of a national prison system and a professional police force, can be described as progressive or an attempt to regulate the behaviour of the 'criminal' or 'dangerous' classes has been a source of much debate. The emergence of a 'history from below' in the 1960s challenged the uncritical reliance on the accounts of the elites offered by 'Whig' historians, putting forward 'revisionist' accounts that questioned the march of progress by drawing attention to the vested interests at play. For example, rather than imprisonment being seen as a progressive approach to punishment in contrast to measures such as corporal punishment and transportation, the history of the prison and prison reform became an analysis of the exercise of power and authority, drawing on and reinforcing existing inequalities (for an introduction to the history of imprisonment, see Muncie, 2001b).

The New Labour governments from 1997 to 2010 deepened and widened the project of further criminalisation. During this period, crime was connected with a range of different areas of social life including education and housing. For Rodger (2008a) this is indicative of one of two key processes that can be described as the criminalisation of social policy. The first, which we return to in Chapter Four, refers to boundary blurring between the goals of welfare and punishment when welfare-oriented agencies work in partnership with criminal justice ones. The second – and the most relevant here – is the displacement of goals; in essence, crime control becomes the goal of social policy interventions as criminal justice solutions are sought to social problems. From this perspective social policy 'abandons its implicit role in ameliorating the conditions that cause criminality and instead becomes an explicit instrument of criminal justice strategy' (Rodger, 2008a: 18). Examples are numerous and include anti-social behaviour generally, drug use (see Chapter Six), nuisance neighbours, truancy (see ***Box 2.1*** below) and rough sleeping (see ***Box 2.3***).

Box 2.1: The criminalisation of truancy

Until the late 1990s, criminologists were interested in truancy because it seemed to be a significant risk factor for involvement in crime (Farrington, 2007; McAra, 2004) rather than a form of crime in its own right. Truancy was perceived to be a welfare matter and largely the responsibility of local education authorities. Measures contained in the Crime and Disorder Act 1998 were therefore highly significant in that they brought truancy under the realm of criminal justice. Police officers were empowered to take action against a young person in a public place if they believed them to be under school leaving age and absent from school without good reason. Officers were permitted to return the young person to a place designated by the local authority, usually the allocated school, and crucially not a police station. Introducing this measure paved the way for further ones, many of which aim to promote 'parental responsibility' such as 'voluntary' parenting contracts for parents of those who fail to attend, with the threat of sanctions if they fail to comply (see Grover, 2008, and Chapter Seven), introduced in the Anti-social Behaviour Act 2003. Sanctions for refusing to sign a contract or non-compliance range from 'on-the-spot' fines (discussed in more detail on pp 14-15) for parents (which can have a significant impact on low-income parents) through to what Fionda (2005: 226) describes as the 'trump card' of prosecution, a fine of up to £2,500 and/or three months' imprisonment. Alongside measures focused on parents, young offenders have increasingly been required to attend school as a condition of an order imposed by the youth justice system or an Anti-social Behaviour Order (ASBO) (see Fionda, 2005). Again, failure to comply can result in further action, leading to criminal sanctions being imposed on young people who engage in truancy, effectively criminalising non-attendance at school. Whether such measures are conciliatory or punitive because they combine 'carrots' (for example, support for parenting) with 'sticks' (for example, fines) has been the source of much debate (see Payne, 2003). Certainly, policies that focus on parenting, such as those designed to tackle truancy, have proved controversial in that they have had a disproportionate effect on mothers (Ghate and Ramella, 2002; Scourfield and Drakeford, 2002). Writing before the new measures were introduced, Wardhaugh (1991) commented on the difficulties stemming from a dual approach of using punishment-oriented education legislation and welfare-oriented child law to tackle truancy. Bringing truancy into the criminal justice policy arena can only heighten the problematic nature of the response. The introduction of new policies to tackle truancy illustrates vividly the tensions that develop when crime control and social policy intersect.

The New Labour governments created quasi-criminal acts defined as 'disorderly' and/or 'anti-social', for which perpetrators would typically be dealt with via 'summary justice'. Summary justice has multiple meanings within English Law (see Morgan, 2008), but in this instance it refers to circumventing traditional routes to justice in favour of expedient disposals that bypass the criminal courts and may not even involve visiting a police station. The aim is to respond in a timely, proportionate and effective manner to relatively minor offences, which do not form part of a pattern of persistent offending. In so doing, it is hoped that criminal justice professionals will be able to expedite dealing with serious offences, with positive benefits for defendants and cost-savings for the criminal justice system. One of the best-known examples of the new form of summary justice is the penalty notice for disorder, known colloquially as an 'on-the-spot' fine. This was introduced by the Criminal Justice and Police Act 2001. ***Box 2.2*** details the list of offences that can be punished with a fine of up to £80. They include acts that the majority of people would regard as criminal (for example, criminal damage or shoplifting) alongside those that would not be viewed in this way (for example, littering and setting off fireworks late at night). Using the same penalties to punish both criminal and non-criminal acts blurs the boundaries between acts that are criminal and those that are variously described as anti-social, disorder or nuisance behaviours. Failing to pay the required amount within 21 days can lead to criminal prosecution so that in effect offences such as littering have become quasi-criminal acts.

Box 2.2: Examples of offences that could result in a penalty notice for disorder

The offences below are those that attract the upper tier penalty – £80 for 16-year-olds and over or £40 for 10- to 15-year-olds:

- Knowingly give a false alarm to a person acting on behalf of a fire and rescue authority
- Use words/conduct likely to cause fear of harassment, alarm or distress
- Drunk and disorderly in a public place
- Destroying or damaging property (under £300, and may only be issued on one occasion)
- Retail theft (under £100, and may only be issued on one occasion)
- Possession by a person under 18 of an adult firework
- Sells or attempts to sell alcohol to a person who is drunk
- Sale of alcohol anywhere to a person under 18
- Buys or attempts to buy alcohol on behalf of a person under 18

- Possess a controlled drug of Class B - cannabis/cannabis resin (use only for persons over 18).

A further six offences, mostly relating to alcohol, attract the lower-tier penalties, which are £50 and £30 respectively (a full list is available at www.homeoffice. gov.uk/police/penalty-notices/).

In some respects the use of summary justice is not a new development since fixed penalty notices have been widely used to respond to minor motoring offences following the Road Traffic Act 1988. What is new is the range of mechanisms now available for both young and adult offenders, and the array of offences for which they can be administered, which has led to mounting concerns about their use, coalescing around the theme of fairness (for an overview, see Morgan, 2008).

Defining threats to order

Just 11 months after forming a government, the Labour Party introduced the Crime and Disorder Bill to the House of Commons. Three months later it was enacted, just over a year after New Labour assumed power. In the run-up to the 1997 General Election the Labour Party, under the leadership of Tony Blair – a former shadow Home Secretary – centred its law and order campaign round the political statement 'tough on crime, tough on the causes of crime'. In this way, it distanced itself from accusations of being 'soft on crime' associated with 'Old' Labour, transforming law and order policies from Labour's 'Achilles heel' (Morgan and Hough, 2007: 46) to one of its perceived strengths (Solomon et al, 2007). New Labour was highly critical of rising record crime rates during the Conservative administrations, despite significant falls in the previous five years (Downes and Morgan, 2012), and outlined an ambitious, and expensive, programme of work in order to reduce crime and to enhance community safety. Beginning with the Crime and Disorder Act 1998, the New Labour government moved quickly to 'instil a new sense of order in society' (Solomon et al, 2007: 17). This Act is now seen as New Labour's flagship legislation. Comprising of 121 sections, it was wide-ranging in terms of its specific provisions covering offences as diverse as racial violence, football hooliganism, rape and homicide, and all aspects of the criminal justice process from the use of police powers through to the release of prisoners. The preamble from the Act illustrates its scope:

> To prevent crime and disorder; to create certain racially-aggravated offences; to abolish the rebuttable presumption that a child is incapable of crime and to make provision as to the

effect of a child's failure to give evidence at his trial; to abolish the death penalty for treason and piracy; to make changes to the criminal justice system; to make further provision for dealing with offenders; to make further provision with respect to remands and committals for trial and the release and recall of prisoners.

Essentially, its main purpose was 'to tackle crime and disorder and help create safer communities' (Home Office, 1998a: 1). There were three underlying themes: making the youth justice system more effective in preventing (re)offending; to promote partnership working between police forces and local authorities; and to ensure that public bodies (including local authorities) reflected on the likely impact of the decisions they made (for example, in relation to planning) on levels of crime and disorder (Home Office, 1998a). Exploring the Act in detail here is beyond the scope of this book (on community safety and crime reduction, see Matthews and Pitts, 2001; Moss and Stephens, 2005; Squires, 2006; on youth justice, see Smith, 2007; Souhami, 2007), and we can only reflect on some of the most important provisions. Later in this chapter we consider the introduction of ASBOs, community-based civil orders backed up by criminal sanctions, which aim to protect individuals and communities from harmful, anti-social acts. In the following two chapters we explore how the range of players involved in developing and implementing crime policy has increased since the Act was introduced. Most significantly, the Act enhanced the role of local authorities in relation to crime control, requiring them to share responsibility with the police for formulating and implementing evidence-based crime and disorder reduction strategies in collaboration with probation, health authorities and representatives from the private and voluntary sectors. Replicating this model of partnership working, the Act also required local authorities – due to their social services and education responsibilities – to establish multi-agency Youth Offending Teams, whose work was to be guided by an annual youth justice plan.

The Act created a vision of an 'orderly' society, defining particular groups such as young people, inadequate parents, problem drug users and sex offenders as a threat to that vision. Again it is possible to trace continuities with the past. In the 19th century 'the dangerous classes' came to represent a multiple threat to order (Graham and Clarke, 2001). Living in insanitary, overcrowded housing and struggling to 'make ends meet' through insecure employment, begging and other forms of crime, the lives of this diverse group contrasted greatly with the Victorian values the middle and upper classes aspired to based on the principles of strict morality and self-reliance. As a result this group were categorised as a threat to public health, public order, moral order, legal order and more generally as a threat to social and economic progress (Graham and Clarke, 2001). The city, where the 'dangerous classes' lived, became synonymous with crime, when arguably the greatest harms related to the appalling living conditions this group had to endure and stemmed from persistent poverty in an era without the safety net of the welfare state. In particular, vagrancy laws were extended in the early part of the 19th century that widened state powers through the inclusion of new offences (Barrett and Harrison, 1999). The Vagrancy Act 1824 – which has been amended several times following its enactment – was introduced to punish 'idle and disorderly persons and rogues and vagabonds in England', making it illegal for individuals to sleep rough or beg on the streets of England and Wales. Parts of the Act – as discussed in ***Box 2.3*** – are still in force today. This provides a reminder that deepening and widening the process of criminalisation does not always require new legislation but can involve 'dusting off' that which had lain dormant.

Box 2.3: The criminalisation of rough sleeping

Under New Labour, rough sleeping quickly became a political priority. Rough sleepers were one of the first groups targeted by the newly created Social Exclusion Unit. Initially based in the Cabinet Office, this cross-departmental unit aimed to provide a 'joined-up' response to tackle social exclusion. Its influential report (Social Exclusion Unit, 1998) led to the creation of a Rough Sleepers Unit. It included an ambitious target of reducing rough sleeping by two thirds by 2002 in its strategy entitled *Coming in from the cold* (Rough Sleepers Unit, 1999). As arguably 'the most visible manifestation of social exclusion', the desire to reduce rough sleeping was understandable, and significant resources were invested to support those judged most 'deserving' to move away from street homelessness (Grover, 2008: 167). Against this backdrop of promoting the social inclusion of rough sleepers, there is evidence of increasing criminalisation of rough sleepers.

In 2011, Westminster Council in London abandoned its plans to introduce a by-law to make rough sleeping in Victoria an offence following an extensive public consultation. Westminster – which has by far the highest number of rough sleepers of any local authority (CLG, 2012a) – was the first to propose additional legislation. Most local authorities either made use of vagrancy laws that date back almost two centuries to arrest those begging or sleeping rough and/or selected from the 'toolkit' of measures designed to address anti-social behaviour. These 'hard' forms of enforcement were typically coupled with 'softer' forms such as controlled drinking zones (which prohibit drinking in public areas) and environmental design measures (for example, benches which are almost impossible to sleep on) (Johnsen and Fitzpatrick, 2007). Collectively, these measures can be understood as an attempt

> to manage rough sleeping and associated behaviours through rendering it less visible (see also May et al, 2005).

For the most part the city is no longer perceived as a 'dangerous' place in the way it was in Victorian England. Many cities have undergone what Atkinson and Helms (2007) describe as an attempt to secure an 'urban renaissance': new shopping centres have been constructed, derelict industrial buildings in inner city areas have been brought back into use as apartments and the night-time economy has grown rapidly. Cities have re-invented themselves as sites of consumption, leisure and places to live. This has extended beyond the city centre and its environs; for example, out-of-town 'parks' have been built where people can shop and enjoy leisure facilities such as cinemas, bowling alleys or restaurants, and private housing estates have been built to create new suburbs. Regenerated post-industrial cities continue to be closely connected to crime. The consumerism of late capitalism, so vividly displayed in the shop windows, can be viewed as criminogenic when coupled with the growth of inequality (see Young, 1999; Hayward, 2004). As noted in the previous chapter, this was offered as an explanation of the UK riots that took place in August 2011. Moreover, as discussed below, the processes of physical and social renewal have attempted to create order through processes of criminalisation.

In the daytime, city centres appear to be orderly places. An abundance of security measures are in place to create order, including CCTV cameras on the streets and private security guards in shops and offices. These have become such routine features of life in late-modern societies that they fade into the background, and people engage in their routine activities with little awareness that they are subject to continuous surveillance. In contrast, at night the city is seen as disorderly: television channels relay a constant diet of reality programmes focused on the drunken, and sometimes violent, behaviour of consumers of the night-time economy, and policy attention is focused on trying to restore order to city streets (see, for example, Home Office, 2011a). This policy attention has been accompanied by considerable academic research which has attempted to understand alcohol-related violence and disorder (see, for example, Winlow and Hall, 2006) and measures taken to prevent it which focus on individuals, places and licensed premises (see, for example, Hadfield et al, 2009).

A recurring theme across these policy developments is the way in which policies that attempt to create order have become as much about exerting social control through the regulation of behaviour as creating better places to live, work or enjoy leisure time. While the search for order has the potential to affect us all, it is felt disproportionately by those groups who are judged to pose a threat to order, for example, young people. Most infamously those wearing hooded tops (predominantly young people) were banned from the Bluewater shopping and leisure complex in 2005, sparking off a moral debate about whether these seemingly innocuous items of fashion clothing had become symbols of fear (Hinsliff et al, 2005). This policy decision utilises the 'precautionary principle' (for a discussion of this concept, see Sunstein, 2005). Rather than responding reactively to the behaviour of individuals by excluding them, it uses a pre-emptive and preventive logic based on the perceived threat posed by specific groups. In this way it attempts to deter behaviour that would otherwise lead to exclusion, backed up with the ability to take action if necessary. In so doing, particular groups are required to regulate their behaviour or face the consequences. Such policies also have wider ramifications because certain categories of people are judged in terms of what they might do rather than what they have done, fuelling negative stereotypes about this group. There was some evidence that the public agreed with the action taken at Bluewater. Immediately following the ban – part of a wider zero tolerance approach to address behaviour judged to be intimidating – visitor numbers rose sharply (BBC News, 2005). This is perhaps unsurprising given the close association between young people and troublesome behaviour in the public's mind (Hough and Roberts, 2004) that such measures could only reinforce. But there are, of course, different ways of interpreting this finding, and the ban may have been counter-productive in that it made the environment attractive to those who wished to enjoy the 'deviant' identity associated with wearing banned forms of clothing.

Critical reflection on both the Crime and Disorder Act 1998 and subsequent measures which have attempted to create 'order' raise the question: whose vision of an 'orderly' society is the driving force behind the plethora of policy initiatives? As **Box 2.4** illustrates, the players involved in the creation of order are many and varied, bringing together the potentially conflicting interests of business, criminal justice and other state and voluntary sector agencies. We return to this theme in the next two chapters when we turn our attention to the crime policy process. For now, we focus on the different interpretations they might have of threats to order.

Box 2.4: Drug use as a threat to order in contemporary cities

Contemporary cities aim to provide an attractive and safe environment for people to shop, eat and drink, or go to the theatre or cinema. Creating safe, orderly and attractive spaces is essential to encourage members of the public to make use of the facilities and to encourage commercial organisations to provide them. Following on from this, certain individuals – and particularly when they are in groups – are perceived to be a threat. Here we focus on problem drug users and highlight some of the key findings from a study that focused on the street policing of this group (Lister et al, 2008). Other groups might encompass those who sleep rough or beg (as described in **Box 2.3**), which also includes problem drug users.

The problem drug users interviewed were 'policed' not only by the public police but individuals working for other statutory and private sector organisations, including municipal wardens, CCTV operators and private security guards. Many of the encounters described by these policing personnel and problem drug users were not reactions to specific incidents of crime. Instead, problem drug users were regularly stopped and asked to account for their presence, were only sometimes searched and were rarely arrested. Exclusionary strategies (both formal and informal) were more commonly deployed to displace problem drug users who were judged to be 'out of place' in contemporary cities. As suggested below, this may be due to their very presence rather than their actual behaviour.

> It appeared often that the presence of certain types of individuals in particular areas was seen as an affront in itself or a type of "symbolic violation". Individuals with what were considered to be the characteristic appearance of many problem drug users encountered on the streets – unkempt, dirty, poorly clothed, emaciated, looking unhealthy – were in effect the human equivalent of Wilson and Kelling's famous "broken windows" (1982). As such, they were perceived as a sign of neighbourhood decline and hence considered to be appropriate targets for policing attention and action, regardless of what they were actually doing. (Lister et al, 2008: 30-1)

The implications of this exclusionary approach can be negative, potentially threatening their links with services working to support them to become drug-free.

The full report can be found at www.jrf.org.uk/publications/street-policing-problem-drug-users

Constructing the anti-social

Political interest in anti-social behaviour developed during John Major's period of office as Prime Minister (1990–97). Launching his Back to Basics campaign at the annual party conference in 1993, he stressed the importance of uniting the divided Conservative Party with 'common-sense British values' (MacIntyre, 1993). Emphasising the need for the 'old core values' of 'neighbourliness, decency and courtesy' along with 'self-discipline and respect for the law' in order 'to defeat the cancer that is crime', Major attempted to appeal to both his political colleagues and the electorate through making a nostalgic plea to return to a, perhaps more imagined than real, golden age. While dismissed by Labour in opposition as a 'cheap electioneering stunt', they adopted a similarly puritanical approach (Presdee, 2009: 216), prioritising it in the 1997 General Election campaign. Inspired by policy developments in the US centred on a commitment to zero tolerance, they focused initially on enhancing community safety. 'Nuisance' behaviours were redefined as 'anti-social' ones (Hodgkinson and Tilley, 2011), taking forward a political concern which Tony Blair had spoken about since 1988 (Solomon et al, 2007).

The term 'anti-social' has been described as a 'problem' largely invented by New Labour (Solomon et al, 2007), although this over-emphasises the discontinuities with the previous government discussed above. Certainly, it became one of their priorities and they were the first to attempt to define it in the Crime and Disorder Act 1998 as acting 'in a manner that caused or was likely to cause harassment, alarm or distress to one or more persons not of the same household as himself'. The use of gendered language in legislation is simply custom and practice, but like crime generally, males are more likely to engage in and be sanctioned for behaving anti-socially (see Moffitt et al, 2001). This definition is both vague and subjective. It defines anti-social behaviour with regard to its effects on others rather than the actual behaviour (Presdee, 2009), and there have been calls to move towards 'greater prescription and definition' (MacKenzie et al, 2010). It allows a wide range of behaviours and incidents to be included, which the Home Office typology (Home Office, 2004a) categorises in terms of the misuse of public space (drug use and dealing, street drinking, begging, prostitution, kerb crawling and sexual acts); disregard for community and personal wellbeing, to include both rowdy and nuisance behaviour; acts directed at people involving intimidation and harassment; and environmental damage involving criminal damage/vandalism and litter/rubbish. The extent to which these are perceived as harmful is a matter for individual interpretation. Blurring the boundaries further, some of the acts included in typology include evidently criminal acts such as joyriding, and arguably some of the most serious offences such as drug dealing. It is worth noting that many of them relate to activities predominantly associated with young people (Presdee, 2009).

The Crime and Disorder Act 1998 introduced ASBOs, which the police or local authorities can apply for against individuals or groups of individuals who engage in persistent and serious anti-social behaviour. These orders have become so infamous that the acronym 'ASBO' is not confined to conversation among criminal justice professionals but has entered the public's vocabulary. These orders blur the boundaries between 'criminal' and 'non-criminal' acts because they can be used for criminal, as well as what the Home Office (1998a: 4) refer to as 'sub-criminal', acts. The orders are reactive in the sense that they aim to put an end to behaviour perceived to be harmful, but also preventative in nature because they must run for a minimum of two years and the threat of criminal sanctions (up to five years' imprisonment) is in place for breaching an order. Consequently, these orders have been described as 'civil-criminal' orders that can be 'hugely penal' if breached (Sanders, 2011: 14). ASBOs are beset with implementation problems, which have been explored elsewhere. They have proved to be particularly controversial because of their high breach rate (Solomon et al, 2007) and because of their disproportionate use for young people, despite initial reassurances that they would be used mainly against adults (Clarke et al, 2011).

ASBOs form part of a wider agenda designed to tackle anti-social behaviour and form its 'cornerstone' (Hodgkinson and Tilley, 2011: 283), and providing an all-encompassing overview of all measures introduced to address anti-social behaviour is not possible here. Alongside the Crime and Disorder Act 1998, which introduced the ASBO and Parenting Orders (see Chapter Seven), the Anti-social Behaviour Act 2003 is a key piece of legislation. Not only did it make changes to existing anti-social behaviour interventions (for example, it introduced CrASBOs, Criminally sought Anti-social Behaviour Orders, which can be served on those convicted of a criminal offence), it also introduced the Dispersal Order which allows the police, working in conjunction with the local authority, to disperse groups of people (which, in the context of the Act, means two or more people) who are behaving anti-socially or who are expected to behave anti-socially. Those dispersed may not be permitted to return to an area – which must have been designated as a dispersal zone in advance – for up to 24 hours, and failing to comply can lead to a fine of up to £5,000 and/or a custodial sentence of up to three months (for a more detailed overview about how the Dispersal Order powers operate in both England and Wales, and Scotland, see Crawford and Lister, 2007). In practice, these powers are used in relation to young people, potentially criminalising this group on the basis of assumptions about what they *might* do rather than their actual behaviour, thus infringing their individual rights (Crawford and Lister, 2007).

The focus on anti-social behaviour continued after 2003. The Respect Agenda emerged during the 2005 General Election campaign and began in 2006 during Blair's third term of office. Launched in January 2006 with a high profile media campaign involving ministers from across government, the Respect Agenda aimed to put the law-abiding majority back in charge of their communities (Blair, 2006). It offers a vivid illustration of New Labour's attempts to 'join up' crime and social policy. While the reduction of anti-social behaviour was its primary aim, its focus was far broader than introducing new criminal justice and civil justice measures, although some were included. Among the 42 actions included in the *Respect Action Plan* (Respect Task Force, 2006) were those related to parenting (particularly addressing 'problem families', as discussed in Chapter Seven), working with young people, improving school attendance and behaviour within schools and strengthening communities. In essence, the *Respect Action Plan* outlined a wide-ranging array of interventions, which it was hoped would address the risk factors for anti-social behaviour in ways that would have wider benefits for individuals, families and communities. The underlying theme, as with many New Labour policies, was emphasising the importance of individuals fulfilling their responsibilities (as citizens, parents and members of communities) in exchange for the rights of citizenship (discussed further in the final chapter). Their responsibilities were described in terms of fulfilling particular duties, for example, ensuring their children attended school, as well as responsibilities to behave in respectful ways. Throughout the *Respect Action Plan* promises of support are coupled with promises to discipline those who continue to behave anti-socially. One example of the tough approach is the threat of eviction to manage the anti-social behaviour caused by 'neighbours from hell'.

While the Respect Agenda has been described as a 'flagship' policy (Tempest, 2006, http://www.guardian.co.uk/politics/2006/jan/10/ immigrationpolicy.ukcrime), criticisms of it are many and varied. It has attracted disapproval from across the political spectrum, ranging from those on the Left concerned about the implications for individual rights of increasing criminalisation, through to those on the Right who argue that it is too tokenistic and law enforcement should be prioritised.

The Respect Agenda was led by the Respect Task Force (headed up by Louise Casey, whose influence on policy-making is described on pp 30-1), which Gordon Brown disbanded in 2007 shortly after becoming Prime Minister. However, much of its work was continued in different guises. This is illustrated in Chapter Seven, which charts how successive governments have incorporated working with families into their crime policies.

The Coalition government has retained the policy emphasis on anti-social behaviour, not least because for a small yet significant proportion of the population (14 per cent in the 2010/11 British Crime Survey), anti-social behaviour is still perceived to be 'fairly big' or a 'very big' problem in their area (Innes, 2011). In an attempt to distance themselves from the measures introduced by New Labour, the Coalition government announced plans to introduce alternative sanctions (see Home Office, 2011b), which would effectively replace the plethora of anti-social behaviour tools with a more streamlined package of wholly civil sanctions. Given the high level of public concern about anti-social behaviour and the apparent failures of New Labour's approach, particularly in the aftermath of the Pilkington case (which involved a mother who killed herself and her severely disabled daughter following repeated harassment by young people upon which the police failed to act), it is perhaps inevitable that the Coalition government would attempt to put 'clear blue water' between their approach and New Labour's. Whether this has been achieved in practice is a moot point. The Coalition government's proposals have been criticised as offering little more than 'old wine in new bottles' by Hodgkinson and Tilley (2011), who go on to argue that there might be greater merits in 'rehabilitating' the existing tools, in particular offering an enhanced level of support to accompany enforcement.

Summary

- In recent years there has been a deepening and widening of the processes of criminalisation. This reflects a historic trend of defining social problems as problems of crime.
- The project of greater criminalisation is linked to the complex process of enhancing social control in late-modern societies characterised by the search for order and security. It fulfils a symbolic role in reassuring the public that community safety is a government priority.
- The creation of new crimes and quasi-crimes provides strategies for controlling the behaviour of individuals in both public and private space, and also serves to control segments of the population, particularly young people, the poor and the socially excluded.

Questions for discussion

- Can you identify further examples of social problems that have been redefined as problems of 'crime'? Why do you think they have been defined in this way?
- Why do criminologists attach so much significance to the Crime and Disorder Act 1998?
- What evidence is there that society is becoming increasingly governed through crime?
- In preparation for reading the next two chapters, try to identify the main players in the development and delivery of crime policy.

Further reading

- Cook, D. (2006) *Criminal and social justice*, London: Sage Publications – examines the relationship between social inequality, crime and criminalisation in both theory and practice.
- Millie, A. (ed) (2009) *Securing respect: Behavioural expectations and anti-social behaviour in the UK*, Bristol: The Policy Press – a collection of essays which reflect on the origins, interpretations and future of New Labour's Respect Agenda.
- Rodgers, J. (2008) *Criminalising social policy: Anti-social behaviour and welfare in a de-civilised society*, Cullompton: Willan Publishing – explores the contemporary politics of social policy and criminalisation.
- Squires, P. (ed) (2008) *ASBO nation: The criminalisation of nuisance*, Bristol: The Policy Press – this volume reflects critically on the origins, application and impact of the 'tools' used to manage anti-social behaviour.

Guide to electronic resources

- The **Centre for Crime and Justice Studies** is an independent charity concerned with both criminal and social justice. Its project entitled 'Harm and Society' encouraged critical reflection on the relationship between crime and social policy: www.crimeandjustice.org.uk/completedprojects.html
- The **European Group for the Study of Deviance and Social Control** (www.europeangroup.org) brings together academics, practitioners and activists who share critical perspectives on crime (broadly defined) and its control.
- *The Guardian* website on the Crime and Disorder Act 1998 (www.guardian.co.uk/commentisfree/libertycentral/2009/jan/13/crime-disorder-act) contains many useful links to related legislation and stories.
- The government's website on **anti-social behaviour**: www.direct.gov.uk/en/CrimeJusticeAndTheLaw/CrimePrevention/DG_4001652

three

Crime policy-making: a myriad of influences

Overview

This chapter explores the myriad of influences on crime policy. It draws on the framework of Hudson and Lowe (2009) to note macro-, meso- and micro-level influences on crime policy-making and to facilitate analysis of the role played by events, individuals, organisations, the public and the media in crime policy-making. It emphasises how this multiplicity of influences can be both complementary and contradictory by using brief case studies from across the different spheres of crime policy. Further examples are explored in Chapters Five, Six and Seven. This chapter offers breadth rather than depth – focusing on some of the most significant influences – and seeks to direct readers to more specialist literature. It focuses on policy development and should be read in conjunction with the next chapter that is oriented more towards policy implementation. At the same time, it is important to appreciate that there is not a clear-cut distinction between these two stages of the policy process, which is explored in the introduction to the literature on policy-making that follows.

Key concepts

Evidence, extra-parliamentary processes, privatisation, managerialism, media, policy transfer, public, scandal, street-level bureaucracy

A brief introduction to policy-making

In this chapter, we focus on government policy-making, which can involve making decisions in response to particular events (see the later section on the role of scandals in the policy-making process), the development of new legislation or changes to existing laws, or the introduction of a set of proposals with an overarching aim (see, for example, the Crime Reduction Programme discussed later in this chapter in **Box 3.3**). The danger with this approach is that it can give the misleading impression that policy-making is 'top down', with power and control invested in those who initiate the proposals and take responsibility for their execution (for example, politicians and senior civil servants). If we adopt a more catholic approach to defining policy – as advocated in the introductory chapter – we recognise that many policies are not initiated at the highest levels but result from those directly involved in crime control. One example here is the scheme introduced by the police in Lambeth to deal with cannabis possession without arrest (see Chapter Six). Local developments work within parameters developed at a national level. Of particular relevance in this respect is the increased emphasis on performance as the principles of new public managerialism (NPM) became central to the work of criminal justice agencies, along with public sector organisations more generally, from the 1980s onwards. Increasingly, local practices were centrally controlled through the imposition of key performance targets and indicators, leading critics to argue that what gets measured gets done (see Chapter Four).

Even when focusing on policy-making initiated at the 'top' it is important to recognise the pivotal role played by 'street-level bureaucrats' (Lipsky, 1980). In the context of crime policy, this term describes not only the 'usual suspects' working within criminal justice agencies such as the police and the courts, but an ever-growing range of players from across the public, private and voluntary sector. These themes are developed further in the next chapter. It is highly likely that street-level bureaucrats will not implement the policy in the way it was intended, so the transfer of policy from 'paper' to 'practice' might lead to unintended consequences. A good illustration in this respect is the introduction of new community penalties. These are often intended for those individuals at risk of receiving a custodial sentence but typically have the effect of being used as a 'tougher' penalty for those who would ordinarily have received another community sanction. This may arise from a deliberate strategy to adapt, or even undermine, a policy, but it can also result from more pragmatic factors, for example, relating to whether sufficient resources are available. The ultimate outcome might be to reconsider the policy. Recognising this, Hudson and Lowe (2009: 245) argue 'policy can be and usually is remade during implementation'.

This brief discussion of the policy process raises questions about how we might attempt to characterise it. Reference is often made to a 'cycle', but on closer inspection this appears to be problematic even as a metaphor rather than an accurate reflection of the realities of policy-making. It over-emphasises the degree of rationality involved in the policy process and fails to appreciate the impact of events. It underestimates the agency of street-level bureaucrats and the complexity of policy networks. Hudson and Lowe (2009) deploy the metaphor of a 'mess' in their analysis of policy-making. For these political scientists, understanding the policy process requires analysis at macro, meso and micro levels. The first relates to broader issues that shape the wider context in which policy is made. In so doing, they emphasise the importance of appreciating that we live in post-industrial societies in a highly globalised world characterised by rapid technological change. They also highlight the significance of understanding the distribution of political power. At the other extreme, at the micro level, they attach great significance to the role of individuals, both in terms of policy-making and implementation, and in so doing they recognise the importance of personalities and the central role played by street-level bureaucrats. This helps to appreciate that individuals are active agents, exerting control over their working lives, but at the same time they are constrained in what they do. Given this tension within policy-making, Hudson and Lowe (2009: 11) advocate the importance of meso-level analysis to appreciate how 'meso-level institutions and networks are crucial in that they filter the impact of macro trends'. This requires us to consider how policies are made, which ones reach the policy agenda and why, and structural arrangements through which policy is developed and implemented.

Political influences

In the previous two chapters we explored the politics of law and order, but to date our focus has been on party politics and the role of politicians. Even if we restrict our focus to government policy-making as detailed above, it is still necessary to appreciate the other key political influences, both within and without government. In so doing we need to reflect on the role of individuals (which requires micro-level analysis) and structural arrangements (which requires macro-level analysis). The section below explores examples of these, paying particular attention to those who role in crime policy-making is often overlooked.

Civil servants

The Civil Service has changed significantly during the past three decades, not least because large government departments have been broken up. The redefining of Home Office responsibilities, leading to the creation of the Ministry of Justice in 2007 alongside the Home Office, provides an illustration of this. Both departments have responsibilities that extend beyond crime policy. The work of the Ministry of Justice spans civil, family and criminal justice (with particular responsibility for courts, prisons and probation), while the Home Office is the lead government department for immigration, alongside policing and drugs policy. It remains the case that both government departments employ significant numbers of civil servants, whose role in crime policy formulation is rarely acknowledged (for a notable exception, see Faulkner, 2001).

The Civil Service describes itself on its website as 'supporting the Government in developing and implementing its policies, and in delivering public services', and identifies its core values as integrity, honesty, objectivity and impartiality (Civil Service, 2010). The extent of its influence on policy-making is a moot point. For Faulkner and Burnett (2011), the influence of the Civil Service has declined, and civil servants have become increasingly required to 'serve' their political 'masters'. Moreover, the rapid movement of civil servants between government departments has resulted in individuals not developing subject-specific knowledge alongside the loss of corporate memory to appreciate, for example, why particular decisions were taken in the past. Overall, 'it can be argued that the civil service has become less valued and less respected as a source of wisdom and expertise, or as an institution with any authority or identity of its own' (Faulkner and Burnett, 2011: 37). While recognising these significant changes it is important not to underestimate the influence of civil servants, who, as Downes and Morgan (2007: 229) argue, 'are far from passive bureaucrats' (for an introductory overview of this debate, see Leach et al, 2011). This chimes with David Faulkner's brief reflections of over 30 years of working for the Home Office. In an article published in *The Guardian* (Faulkner, 2004), he argues that it is the role of civil servants to question, at times, what they have been asked to do by their ministers, who should in turn respect and accept such advice even if they choose not to act on it.

There have been further changes too. Under New Labour, influential civil servants began to undertake a different role. Rather than occupying a low-key presence, largely hidden from view within Whitehall, they actively engaged with the public through the media. Downes and Morgan (2007: 229) argue that this development can be conceptualised as the 'rise of the activist, celebrity servants taking the Prime Minister's message to the country' (see also Morgan, 2006). They suggest that in relation to crime control the most obvious example is Louise Casey, who has occupied high-profile roles under the New Labour governments and the Coalition government. In the space of 13 years, she has headed up the Rough Sleepers Unit, the Anti-social Behaviour Unit and the Respect Task Force (see *page 23* in Chapter Two), and also undertook the role of Victims' Commissioner. She is currently Director-General of the Troubled Families Unit, whose work is explored later in Chapter Seven. Described in the media as an 'outspoken New Labour apparatchik' (Batty, 2008), this rather derogatory conceptualisation does reflect the nature of the role of the 'celebrity' civil servant: they are expected to speak out in ways in keeping with government policy. At this point, it is also worth noting the rise of other 'celebrities' within crime policy-making, who are often relations of murder victims. Examples include Sara Payne, the mother of Sarah Payne who was killed by a known paedophile in 2000, given the position of 'Victim's Champion' for one year in 2009, and Brooke Kinsella, a television actress and the sister of Ben Kinsella who was murdered in 2008, tasked with reviewing local anti-knife crime projects (Kinsella, 2011).

The House of Lords

Also neglected from discussions about formal crime policy-making is the role of the House of Lords, the Second or Upper House of Parliament. The House of Lords has three main roles: to make laws (in conjunction with the House of Commons), to provide in-depth consideration of public policy and to hold governments to account (see www.parliament. uk/business/lords/work-of-the-house-of-lords/what-the-lords-does/). It has a reputation for being 'arcane and archaic' and an 'exemplar of social inequality' (Bochel and Defty, 2010: 367), and at the time of writing, a report on the 2011 draft Bill has just been published (House of Lords/ House of Commons, 2012). The 2011 British Social Attitudes survey found that public attitudes to the House of Lords are mixed: while two fifths are in favour of members of the second chamber being all or mostly elected, there remains substantial support for including at least some appointed members, particularly independent experts (Curtice and Seyd, 2012). The need for reform is recognised by all the political parties, and proposals were included in all their 2010 General Election manifestos. Reform of the House of Lords is, of course, not new, and was undertaken by New Labour who removed the majority of hereditary peers in an attempt to make it more democratic and representative and to enhance its effectiveness and legitimacy (see Stationery Office, 1999; Bochel and Defty, 2010). Despite its reputation it can be influential in terms of 'persuad[ing] the government to make policy changes on a diverse range of issues' including crime-related ones such as the protection of the public's right to trial by jury and making forced marriage illegal. A list of 'defeats' (that is, when it has reversed decisions made in the House of Commons) is maintained at www.ucl.ac.uk/constitution-unit/research/parliament/house-of-lords/ lords-defeats. A number of commentators have argued that it has become more assertive (for example, Russell and Sciara, 2005; Howe, 2007; Bochel and Defty, 2010), and similarly, Bochel and Defty's (2007) research on MPs revealed that they felt the House of Lords was playing a more substantial role in the formulation and scrutiny of social policy and legislation. It is worth noting, however, that the House of Lords sometimes challenges government proposals, even when they have been largely supported by the House of Commons. For example, as we will note in Chapter Six, the House of Lords challenged plans to introduce quasi-compulsory drug treatment for problem drug users wishing to claim benefits when the Welfare Reform Bill 2009 passed to the Upper House after relatively little debate in the House of Commons. On this occasion, one of the crossbenchers (that is, a member [peer] who does not have a connection to any political party) was highly influential in representing the views of the drugs field and medical profession. We explore further the involvement of such individuals (that is, those with expertise and interests in particular issues) in crime policy-making in the remainder of this section on political influences, which focus on extra-parliamentary processes.

Experts and advisers

Experts and advisers can be involved in policy-making in a number of ways. Later in this chapter we consider the role of researchers in gathering evidence, primarily through the evaluation of new initiatives. This section focuses on experts and advisers who have specifically been invited by government to contribute to policy-making on a specific area, either on an ad hoc basis (see the discussion of Royal Commissions below) or on a more ongoing basis (see the discussion of advisory bodies below).

A **Royal Commission** is a group of people selected and appointed by government to investigate a matter of important public concern and to make recommendations on any actions to be taken. They date back to the 19th century, and are only established periodically. Calls for Royal Commissions to be established occur much more frequently. In 2011, John Hemming (a Liberal Democrat MP) raised an Early Day Motion for a Royal Commission on Policing to counter the perceived fragmentary and disconnected approach to police reform. (Early Day Motions are a mechanism whereby a backbench MP can table a motion on any subject and call for a debate.) It was signed by 90 MPs from across the political spectrum. No such Commission was established, but the Labour Party (in opposition) took the unusual step of announcing (via its shadow Home Secretary, Yvette Cooper) that it was establishing its own independent review of 'the crime challenges of the 21st century and how policing needs to adapt and respond' (Cooper, 2011). It is due to report in 2013.

During the past three decades there have been only two Royal Commissions focused on crime and its control. The first, the Royal

Commission on Criminal Procedure, was established in 1978 to examine the investigation and prosecution of criminal offences, with particular reference to the need to balance the rights and liberties of those accused with those of the community in bringing offenders to justice in an efficient and economical way (for brief critical analysis, see Harlow, 1981; Munday, 1981). Reporting three years later, it recommended systematic reform of the criminal investigative process in order to balance the powers and duties of the police with the rights and duties of suspects. In direct response to this, the Police and Criminal Evidence Act 1984 (known colloquially as PACE) was introduced, which laid out a statutory framework for the criminal investigation process. In practical terms, it introduced measures such as tape-recording police interviews, limiting the time a person could be detained without charge and providing suspects with a right to legal representation. The extent to which PACE has had an impact on police behaviour is a source of debate (for an overview, see Brown, 1997), but there is some consensus that it has made the police more accountable for the powers they deploy when conducting investigations (Jones, 2009). The Act also laid the foundations for the development of the CPS, which acts as a second filter (following the police) for making decisions to prosecute based on the criteria of sufficient evidence and public interest (Uglow, 2009).

A more recent example is the Royal Commission on Criminal Justice, which was established in 1991 in the aftermath of the convictions of the 'Birmingham Six' being quashed by the Court of Appeal following 16 years of wrongful imprisonment. Chaired by Viscount Runciman, it was asked to examine the effectiveness of the criminal justice system in England and Wales in securing the conviction of those found guilty of criminal offences and the acquittal of those who were innocent. Part of the process included commissioning research studies (see, for example, Maguire and Norris, 1993). Compared to its predecessor, the extent of the 1991 Commission's influence is less evident (for a brief critical analysis, see Young and Sanders, 1994). On this occasion, the experts involved did not wholly agree, and the final report (Royal Commission on Criminal Justice, 1993) included a Note of Dissent written by one of the members, Professor Michael Zander. It produced over 350 recommendations, which, as Faulkner (2001: 124) notes, 'have generally been adopted'. In this respect it has been successful, but a number of commentators have drawn attention to its overly pragmatic focus and its lack of theoretical depth: Faulkner (2001: 124) likened it to a 'management consultant's review of the criminal justice process', while Lacey (1994b) argued that it focused on the trees but missed the wood; in this instance, wider debate about balancing the rights of suspects and the wider society. By the time the Commission reported, law and order issues had become, as noted in the introductory chapter, heavily politicised. One consequence of this is that the view of experts can be overridden by political concerns. The abolition of the right to silence in the Criminal Justice and Public Order Act 1994, despite the Royal Commission concluding it should be retained (see Sanders et al, 2010), is a vivid illustration of this.

Advisory bodies operate within a different model. They involve experts providing advice on an ongoing basis, although advisers are typically appointed for a fixed-term period. They are examples of quasi-autonomous non-governmental organisations (often referred to as 'quangos'). The term quangos describes a much wider range of organisations than advisory bodies. For example, it also includes consumer 'watchdogs' and organisations that carry out public services. The influence of quangos on policy-making has declined sharply since the Coalition formed a government in May 2010. Only a matter of months later it was announced that almost 200 would either be disbanded completely or their functions undertaken by others. Among the list of those disbanded were several with responsibility for crime control. Most controversially, it included the Youth Justice Board (discussed in the next chapter), a decision reversed a year later in the face of strong opposition. Government departments became the most likely recipients of their work, but also voluntary and community sector bodies, in keeping with the government's pursuit of its 'Big Society' agenda (also discussed in the next chapter). This bold reform was dubbed the 'bonfire of the quangos' by the media in homage to historical events where objects (for example, books or paintings) believed to be sinful were burnt. It was justified by the need to reduce government spending and to enhance accountability since quangos are publicly funded but not controlled by Whitehall.

Advisory bodies are established as independent of government, providing expert advice but not directing policy-making. They may carry out in-depth investigations on particular topics, resulting in the publication of policy-relevant reports. The most well-known, and in some respects infamous and certainly controversial, example of an advisory body focused on crime issues is the Advisory Council on the Misuse of Drugs (see **Box 6.2**). In 2009, the 'sacking' of its chair, Professor David Nutt, ignited a debate about the role of experts in policy-making and the independence of advisory bodies. A further example of an advisory committee working on crime issues is the Crime Statistics Advisory Committee (established in 2011) which has responsibility for ensuring that 'official statistics on crime for England and Wales are accurate, clearly presented, comprehensive, transparent and trustworthy taking account of the needs of users and providers' (UK Statistics Authority, 2012).

Pressure and campaigning groups

Pressure and campaigning groups are influential in crime policy-making, particularly in relation to penal policy. The oldest is the Howard League for Penal Reform, which was established in its current form in 1921, but whose origins can be traced back to the mid-19th century (Ryan, 2003). Pressure groups began to proliferate in the late 1960s (Downes and Morgan, 2007), a time, as already noted, when law and order issues came to the fore again. Often these groups combine their roles of campaigning and lobbying with providing a range of services to either victims or offenders. For example, the Howard League provides legal services to prisoners.

There are numerous differences between pressure and campaigning groups working within the crime policy sphere. First, while all have clearly defined aims, some are more specialist in terms of the issues they seek to bring to the attention of policy-makers. For example, Hibiscus was initially established to campaign for female foreign nationals imprisoned in the UK, although its remit is now wider and includes, for example, women who are European Union (EU) nationals, refugees and asylum-seekers (see Heaven and Hudson, 2005). Second, they vary both in terms of the size of the organisation and the extent to which they are professionalised. The criminal justice field varies from large-scale organisations (for example, Nacro, described on page 92) with teams that perform specialist functions such as media relations through to those that comprise of only of a small number of individuals working on a voluntary basis. Third, they vary in terms of their relationship with government, with some receiving part of their funding from government, typically to provide services. In this way, organisations such as Victim Support have a complex relationship with governments, receiving financial support to provide their services at the same time as being critical of government policy on victims and witnesses. Increasingly, pressure and campaigning groups work collaboratively to heighten their impact, putting aside ideological differences to achieve shared goals in relation to a specific policy issue or more generally. Examples are provided in *Box 3.1*.

Box 3.1: Alliances and coalitions

The **Criminal Justice Alliance** (www.criminaljusticealliance.org) is a coalition of over 60 organisations committed to improving the criminal justice system. Its members include campaigning charities, voluntary sector service providers, research institutions, staff associations and trade unions. Even a cursory glance through the list of members published on its website leads to an appreciation of the diversity of the membership, not only in terms of type of organisation (as detailed above), but in terms of the focus of its work. Many are national organisations but there are exceptions, and smaller voluntary and community sector organisations are represented through Clinks (see below).

Clinks (www.clinks.org) is a national organisation that was founded in 2001, although its history can be traced back to the early 1990s. It supports, represents and campaigns for the voluntary and community sector who work with offenders. It aims to influence decision-makers on behalf of the voluntary and community sector. It plays a key role in representing small and community organisations that may not have the resources to attempt to sway politicians and senior civil servants. To this end, Clinks engages in lobbying, campaigning and preparing formal responses to government consultations and proposals. Clinks often works in partnership with other organisations working in related areas. They were one of a number of organisations and individuals involved in the Transition to Adulthood (T2A) Alliance, described below.

Transition to Adulthood (T2A) Alliance (www.t2a.org.uk) is a coalition of 12 criminal justice, health and youth organisations, convened by the Barrow Cadbury Trust, a charitable foundation whose work supports vulnerable and marginalised young people (see www.bctrust.org.uk). It advocates the need for a tailored approach to working with young adults (that is, those aged 18–20) in the criminal justice system, which takes into account their level of maturity and specific needs. Despite the narrow age range, young adults comprise 14 per cent of offenders sentenced to Community Orders in 2011 (Ministry of Justice, 2012a), and on average 9 per cent of the prison population in England and Wales in the first three months of 2012 (Ministry of Justice, 2012b). The Alliance grew out of the work of a Commission established by the Barrow Cadbury Trust, which reported in 2005 (Barrow Cadbury Trust, 2005). Established in 2008, it has been a prolific producer of research and policy reports and has also piloted a small number of projects with its target group to develop effective ways of working. In March 2012, the Riots Communities and Victims Panel's final report made two concrete recommendations based on evidence included by the T2A Alliance in its submission.

Think tanks

There is no universally agreed definition of think tanks, but in a general sense the term refers to organisations comprising of policy experts who are engaged – to varying extents – in public policy research, advocating policy solutions to problems and lobbying for policy reform. It is anticipated that the latter two roles are informed by the former, so that policies proposed are evidence-based (an issue we return to later in this chapter). Evidence in this instance may not be neutral or gathered systematically through methodologically rigorous research. In the UK, think tanks are often relatively small organisations but with a wide remit. Usually the focus of their work is expressed in terms of an overarching political ideology (for example, a commitment to free market economics) rather a specific policy area. By their very nature they are political entities but are typically non-partisan (a notable exception is the Fabian Society which is allied to the Labour Party), even if the policies they are advocating are remarkably similar to those of a political party. Instead, they are independently funded non-profit making organisations, although often the sources of funding are opaque (Monbiot, 2012). Governments tend to forge close working relationships with a selective few, and Downes and Morgan (2007: 228) argue that think tanks are sometimes viewed as 'extensions of the Cabinet Office, flying kites for ministers to see how the wind of public or elite opinion blows'. They further suggest that this frequently involves announcements on law and order issues. The connection between think tanks and politics becomes even fuzzier if we consider the example of the Centre for Social Justice, which aims to address social breakdown, ameliorate poverty and promote social justice (for a discussion of its work on problem drug use, see Chapter Six, ***Box 6.4***). This was established in 2004 by the current Work and Pensions Secretary (then a backbencher). Its present advisory council includes two Labour MPs (one as chair), two Conservative MPs, one MEP (Cosnervative) and the current Deputy Prime Minister's adviser.

Political influences: a final note

The list of political influences described above is far from comprehensive. Drawing attention to those political influences that are often overlooked was a deliberate strategy but inevitably some have been glossed over. These include the role played by trade unions (for example, the National Association of Probation Officers, the Prison Officers Association and the Police Federation) and professional associations (for example, the Probation Chiefs' Association, Prison Governors Association and Association of Chief Police Officers) and those tasked with identifying the deficiencies within current policy and practice and developing recommendations for change (for example, HM Inspectorates of Prison and Probation).

Looking elsewhere: the importance of policy transfer

Policy transfer is increasingly important to meso-level analysis of the crime policy-making process, but as a concept it lacks a precise meaning and is best referred to as 'a generic, umbrella term that encompasses the many different conceptions of the process by which ideas, institutions, or programmes from one time or place are used in another' (Hudson and Lowe, 2009: 197). Policy transfer typically refers to the transfer of policies from other countries to the UK (see *Box 3.2* for crime-related examples). However, we should note that 'home-grown' policies have been transferred overseas, for example, probation (Worrall and Canton, 2013).

Box 3.2: Examples of policy transfer from overseas

- Electronic monitoring
- Evidence-based policy
- Mandatory sentencing for repeat offenders
- Prison privatisation
- Quasi-compulsory drug treatment for offenders (see Chapter Six)
- Restorative justice
- Sex offender registration
- 'What works' (in the narrow sense of cognitive behavioural programmes for offenders)
- Zero tolerance policing

Almost all the policies listed in *Box 3.2* are understood to have originated in the US and have provided inspiration for policy-makers in England and Wales. This has led commentators to argue that there has been an 'Americanisation' of crime policy, along with social policy more generally, and particularly in relation to social welfare policy (see Jones and Newburn, 2002a, 2002b; Newburn, 2002). The most obvious exception to US influence is restorative justice, whose roots lie in the practices of the Maori communities of New Zealand (for an introduction to the concept and its origins, see Goodey, 2005). Policy transfer can also describe using policies that have operated in different policy spheres and applying them to crime control. The next chapter describes how the Payment by Results (PbR) model currently being introduced across many aspects of criminal justice (including all the policy areas discussed in Chapters Five, Six and Seven) is based in part on approaches that have been deployed in relation to health and welfare-to-work. Finally, it is often not appreciated that policy transfer can involve the reintroduction of policies from the past. Prison privatisation is a good example in this respect. We can trace its recent history back to 1993 (see **Box 4.4**), but this was in some respects resurrecting practices that dated back to the Middle Ages when private individuals built and ran prisons (Cavadino and Dignan, 2006).

The policies above are those *believed to* have origins elsewhere. 'Believed to' is emphasised to draw attention to two issues: first, the lack of evidence that policies have been transferred, and second, debates around policy convergence. We deal with each issue in turn. With some notable exceptions, in particular the work of Trevor Jones and Tim Newburn (see, for example, Jones and Newburn, 2007), criminological literature surrounding the policies above is based on the assumption that policy transfer has taken place, not necessarily direct copying, but at the very least policy-makers have taken inspiration from policies adopted elsewhere (for a discussion of different degrees of transfer, see Dolowitz, 2000). Jones and Newburn (2002b: 116) argue that 'a clear need exists for detailed empirical research to provide concrete evidence about how and why policy has changed'. Their own work on the privatisation of punishment, mandatory sentencing and zero tolerance policing explores the complex processes involved in policy transfer, in particular relative contributions of broader structural forces and human agency to understanding policy development. This is a central debate within contemporary comparative criminology. A number of commentators, most notably Christie (2000) and Garland (2001), have remarked on the many similarities between crime control policies in Western industrialised societies. They cite evidence of rising imprisonment rates, harsher sentencing policies, zero tolerance policing strategies and private sector involvement (what Christie, 2000, refers to as the 'commodification' of crime control) as evidence of convergence to support their claim (Jones and Newburn, 2002b). To make sense of this apparent similarity of crime control strategies, supporters of the policy convergence thesis look to the core structural and cultural characteristics of late-modern, capitalist societies, while also recognising the importance of globalising processes. For Garland (2001) – whose work concentrates on the UK and the US – acceptance of high crime rates, recognition that the state is not solely responsible for crime control, and appreciation of the limits of the criminal justice system in reducing crime have led to 'adaptive strategies' (essentially highly pragmatic responses) alongside the promotion of expressive policies which 'denounce the crime and reassure the public' (Garland, 2001: 176). Examples of the former include electronic monitoring, prison privatisation and sex offender registration. Examples of the latter include mandatory sentencing for repeat offenders and zero tolerance policing. Collectively they form part of a 'culture of control' (Garland, 2001).

Advocates of the policy convergence thesis are careful to steer away from determinism, which would avoid recognising important differences between countries. An obvious example here is imprisonment rates that are far higher in the US, which imprisons 730 citizens per 100,000 population, compared to the UK, which imprisons 155 (International Centre for Prison Studies, 2012). While they emphasise the role of social, economic and political forces, they still appreciate the role played by individuals and organisations that make policy decisions. However, it can be argued that they do not pay sufficient attention to the role of key actors in the policy process, and how globalisation (a macro-level concept) interacts at a micro level with individuals seeking to bring about policy change. Crime is increasingly being recognised as a global phenomenon that crosses national borders (for example, the supply of drugs and human trafficking), sometimes taking place in the 'virtual' space of the internet. Technological change (also highly significant to macro-level policy analysis) has also resulted in a 'contracted' world, allowing policy-makers to become aware of developments in other countries and to communicate easily with their counterparts in other jurisdictions. Under such circumstances it seems likely that they will deliberately and consciously set out to draw lessons from elsewhere or to develop policy networks through which knowledge and experience might be shared. The end result might be something specific such as the transfer of policy content, instruments, programmes and institutions (for example, the Drug Abuse Resistance Education Program) through to the more general: ideologies, ideas, attitudes and policy goals (for example, the language of 'zero tolerance' or welfare-to-work) (see Dolowitz and Marsh, 1996).

An important question to ask when looking at instances of policy transfer is who is involved. This is one of seven questions posed by Hudson and Lowe (2009) who have adapted Dolowitz and Marsh's (1996) influential framework. Hudson and Lowe (2009) distinguish between three broad groupings of players. The first is insiders, which in this instance refers to those inside the political system. An obvious example here is David Cameron's invitation (blocked by the Home Office) to William Bratton, a former Chief of Police in the Los Angeles Police Department, to become the new Metropolitan Police Commissioner. Reductions in crime in Los Angeles following the 1992 riots are often attributed to Bratton's zero tolerance policing approach (see Jones and Newburn, 2007), which Cameron was keen to introduce in the UK following the urban disturbances in August 2011. The second, outsiders, refers to non-governmental organisations (NGOs). This includes think tanks whose activity is at a global level and consequently, such organisations can play a central role in the transfer of policy from other countries, often the US, to England and Wales (Stone,

2001). The Adam Smith Institute (described on page 72) argued strongly that privatisation should be introduced in the UK. Similarly, pressure and campaigning groups are sometimes multinational. One example that works in the field of crime control is Amnesty International, whose remit is also far wider. It has run a long-standing campaign for the abolition of the death penalty. The final grouping – global players – describes supranational governmental organisations and NGO and policy entrepreneurs, experts and consultants. Supranational institutions are now influential both within Europe and beyond, and provide examples of the changing nature of governance (a further component of macro–level policy analysis). These institutions can be influential in promoting consistency of policies across countries. The United Nations (UN) is an illustrative example here: its Office on Drugs and Crime aims to transfer best practice in relation to tackling drugs, trafficking and terrorism (see www.unodc.org/), and the UN Convention on the Rights of the Child similarly aims to promote a 'child first' approach within youth justice across member states. A recent example of the role played by supranational institutions is the debate in the UK about whether prisoners should be entitled to vote. At present, only remand prisoners (those awaiting trial or sentence) are allowed to vote. In contrast, most European countries do not have blanket bans on convicted prisoners being unable to vote, and instead differentiate between prisoners of different sentence length and/or according to their offence. All prisoners in Denmark, Sweden and Switzerland are free to vote. In 2005, the European Court of Human Rights (ECHR) ruled the UK ban unlawful, and in 2010 the Court of Europe, which enforces the ECHR's decrees, requested that the UK government address the situation. This resulted in a House of Commons debate, in which MPs overwhelmingly agreed to defy the ECHR ruling. At the time of writing, the UK government has still not made moves towards compliance despite being issued with a deadline (now in the past) with which to comply.

Evidence-based policy

Examining the role of evidence (more specifically, research evidence) in policy-making is an example of micro–level analysis. If we adopt the view that the policy process is akin to a cycle, it is clear where evidence fits in: the available evidence informs the development of a policy which is then implemented (as intended) and subject to monitoring and evaluation, which can then be used to inform policy decisions, for example, to refine the policy, to develop an alternative approach and so on. As discussed at the beginning of this chapter, the policy process is in reality far messier than this, making it difficult to see where evidence might fit among the many other, seemingly less rational, influences on policy-making. Nonetheless, it is the notion of evidence-based policy that has risen in prominence since 1997. From the late 1990s, there has been growing evidence of what Solesbury (2001: 1) refers to as a 'utilitarian turn' in relation to social science research. This term characterises the changing perception of the role of social science research, and a shared view across research funders, within and without government, that research should not be done for its own sake but should advance social progress. This view has significant implications for the type of research that is funded, shifting the focus from 'basic' (theory-generating research) to 'applied' research (focused on generating practical solutions to problems), which often takes the form of evaluation (for a critical discussion of this dichotomy, see Hammersley, 1995, originally developed by Janowitz, 1972).

As part of its commitment to the modernisation of public services, New Labour argued strongly for the need to develop the information economy and to invest in research in order to gather evidence of 'what works' to ensure that resources were deployed in the most economic, efficient and effective manner. *Box 3.3* describes the Crime Reduction Programme, which represents a practical embodiment of New Labour's apparent commitment to developing evidence-based policy. It includes multiple examples of using 'pilot' or 'pathfinder' approaches to assist with crime prevention, policing and responding to offenders. Accompanied by monitoring and evaluation, the intention of this model was to explore the most effective ways of working in order to establish best practice, which could then be more widely disseminated. The use of a small number of pilots to test innovative ways of working became a standard approach to policy-making under the New Labour government (Cabinet Office, 2003). Examples of using this approach to develop resettlement policy and practice are given in Chapter Five. Pilot projects provide an opportunity to minimise the risk associated with introducing new policies and modes of delivery that have yet to demonstrate they can be effective. If accompanied by rigorous evaluation they can provide evidence of effective practice to inform decisions about whether to 'roll out' interventions on a larger scale, and if so, what changes might need to be made to the initial design. A small-scale embryonic initiative requires a considerable investment of time and resources but reduces the risk – financial and otherwise – of introducing approaches that prove to be ineffective.

There is an extensive literature on evidence-based policy; indeed, this aspect of social policy is represented through specialist journals (for example, *Evidence & Policy*) and dedicated research centres (for example, the Centre for Evidence-based Policy, King's College London). This literature draws attention to the multiple typologies that exist of the relationship between the two. These typologies comprise models that provide a neat way of summarising the multiplicity of relationships between research and policy. The relationships are reflective of reality but can never be a wholly accurate conceptualisation of the messy realities of policy-making. For those new to the field, Young et al's (2002) five-part typology is helpful. The first three relationships in the typology, 'knowledge-driven', 'problem-solving' and 'interactive', focus on the links between research and policy, the first arguing that research leads policy, the second that research follows policy and the third emphasising the two-way relationship between research and policy. New Labour's position initially appears most closely aligned to the second conceptualisation, given that across many policy spheres researchers were commissioned to conduct evaluations of new interventions with the aim of building up a knowledge base about 'what works'. In practice, the relationships were more complex than this implies. Researchers and policy-makers often form 'policy communities' (Young et al, 2002: 216) alongside other stakeholders such as practitioners and users, who, for example, make decisions collectively about research design and the evolution of interventions requiring evaluation so that the boundaries between researcher and policy-maker become blurred. This represents the fourth relationship within the typology.

A recurring theme of the literature on evidence-based policy is the gap – and some would argue that it is a void – between its vision and the realities of policy-making. The Crime Reduction Programme provides a vivid illustration of this. A growing number of social science researchers, which includes a number of criminologists (see, for example, Mair, 2005; Naughton, 2005; Hope and Walters, 2008), have become increasingly sceptical of evidence-based policy as currently practised. As Hudson and Lowe (2009) describe, they are concerned that the evidence is being used in a symbolic fashion to legitimise government decisions, reflecting the final category in Young et al's typology.

Box 3.3: Crime Reduction Programme

The Crime Reduction Programme was launched in 1999 as a 10-year programme (although it ran only for three) to establish 'what works' in relation to 1,500 pilot projects, which would then inform decisions about which projects would be 'scaled up' and implemented nationally. A total of £400 million was earmarked for investment, with £25 million 'ring-fenced' for evaluation that could be used to develop research-based knowledge about the (cost-)effectiveness of the new interventions. The scope of the programme was broad (see Homel et al, 2004). It covered both hidden crimes such as domestic violence and more visible crimes such as burglary and prostitution. Situational crime prevention measures (that is, those which aim to deter individuals from offending by reducing opportunities for them to do so and/or making it more likely that they will get caught) such as CCTV and schemes to provide improved locks for older people were accompanied by social ones working with young people, children and their families perceived to be at risk of offending. Projects involved different stages of the criminal justice process, from arrest through to developing programmes for convicted offenders. In keeping with the aims of the Crime and Disorder Act 1998 (see Chapter Two), the projects were multi-agency, delivered through both formal and informal partnerships (see Chapter Four).

Maguire (2004) argues that the Crime Reduction Programme was ambitious and idealistic, conceived at a time when there was a strong commitment to evidence-based policy. In a useful article in which he compares the vision and reality of the programme, Maguire (2004) draws attention to a range of factors that led to it being terminated early. These include practical implementation problems, cultural issues, changes in the political climate and research-related issues. To understand why the programme 'failed' requires exploration of the complex relations between policy-makers, politicians, practitioners and academic researchers, but in essence, poorly implemented projects led to few conclusive results at a time when politicians were under pressure to reduce crime rates. His overall conclusion is that large-scale and high profile programmes may have less impact on policy than 'a series of quiet iterative processes in individual corners of the criminal justice arena' (Maguire, 2004: 233).

Homel et al (2004) offer an 'official' account of the implementation of the programme. A more critical collection of articles on academics' experiences of evaluating, it was published as a special issue of *Criminology and Criminal Justice* in 2004.

The question that remains is whether evidence-based policy could – and indeed should – ever be achieved given what we know about the complexities of the policy process. The notion of 'evidence-informed' policy is rapidly gaining currency, which does not privilege the role of evidence in policy decisions or over-emphasise its ability to provide definitive answers to the question of 'what works'. Ray Pawson's work has been influential here, arguing that rather than seeking to recommend particular policies, researchers should aim to elucidate context and mechanisms that seem to produce the most desirable outcomes (Pawson, 2002). Ultimately there remains the problem of the clash of researchers emphasising longer-term strategies and 'solutions' while policy-makers are under pressure to seek a 'quick fix' (see Maguire, 2004). Pressure can come from the public and the media, sometimes in response to particular events or 'scandals'. The remainder of this chapter focuses on these issues.

The role of the 'public'

In the heading above the term 'public' is placed in inverted commas to draw attention to its contested meaning. In everyday speech we refer to the public (even using the term the 'general public') in ways that imply that it is an undifferentiated mass (see Hancock, 2004) without recognising the diversity of this group, both in terms of sociodemographic characteristics such as gender, age, ethnic origin and socioeconomic status, but also norms and values. Consequently, when references are made to public opinion, for example, by politicians, they are often referring to those members of the public who are in a position to articulate their view, typically those who are the most literate. *Box 3.4* provides examples of new mechanisms used by governments to garner public opinion generally but also specifically on crime and criminal justice. They form part of an attempt to address what is increasingly referred to as the 'democratic deficit'. Readers should note the increased reliance on technology and the implications of this for excluding particular groups who may not have either the skills to use the available technology or the financial resources to access it with ease. These may be groups who are most fearful of crime (for example, older people) or who experience higher levels of victimisation (for example, those living in poverty) (see Pantazis, 2006).

Box 3.4: Online polls and e-petitions

Policing priorities: An online poll. In 2011, the Home Affairs Committee (a committee appointed by the House of Commons to examine the expenditure, administration and policy of the Home Office and its associated public bodies) established an online poll to gauge public opinion on priorities for policing. It formed part of the Committee's inquiry into the *New landscape of policing*, which was a response to the government's proposal for police reform set out in *Policing in the 21st century* (Home Office, 2010). Members of the public were invited to rank 18 areas of police work as either 'low', 'medium' or 'high' priority. They ranged from dealing with minor crimes such as road traffic offences and criminal damage through to the most serious ones, for example, sexual assault, murder and terrorism. In total, over 20,000 votes were cast, with the public expressing their views most commonly on prostitution, alcohol-related crime and anti-social behaviour. It was also possible to post a comment, but relatively few were received: 271 in total, an average of 15 per topic area. Comments were summarised in the final report (see Home Affairs Committee, 2011).

E-petitions were established by the Coalition government. Described on the website (http://epetitions.direct.gov.uk) as 'an easy, personal way for you to influence government and Parliament in the UK', they allow members of the public to create a petition, which the public can sign online for up to one year after it was posted. Members of the public do not have a free rein because the petition is checked initially by the relevant government department. They must call on the government for a specific action, not substantially duplicate an existing open e-petition, and satisfy the terms and conditions, for example, be submitted by a British citizen or UK resident and to not contain confidential information. At the time of writing, almost half of those submitted have been rejected. If the petition collects 100,000 signatures it can be debated in the House of Common provided that an MP is willing to make the case for consideration to the Backbench Business Committee. E-petitions which are 'trending' (note the use of social media language) are flagged up for the public to see as soon as the website loads. At the time of writing, four of the twelve described as 'trending' related to crime and its control, and it is evident that this vehicle for influencing policy is being used by criminal justice professionals – in this instance, police officers – to trigger debates on police pensions, police reform and the right to strike. To date, only three e-petitions have reached the threshold. Most relevant for readers of this book is the one that advocated the removal of benefits from those convicted for involvement in the London 2011 riots. Whether this was debated in Parliament is somewhat ambiguous. While the Commons Select Committee (2011) maintained that the substance of the e-petition was explored in the debate that took place after Parliament was recalled, media coverage reported that it had been ignored (see, for example, Jackson, 2011).

In relation to crime the 'public' may have very different starting points in terms of their knowledge and understanding of the nature and extent of crime and the processes through which suspects are apprehended and offenders are brought to justice. They may have starkly contrasting views of which crimes are the most serious, the reasons why individuals offend and how crime should be controlled. Finally, they are likely to have diverse experiences of crime, which are shaped by direct victimisation, indirect victimisation (for instance, crimes against their family and friends), media consumption (discussed in the next section) and, for some, experiences of criminal justice as offenders, employees or volunteers. Consequently, while it is possible to identify recurring themes within public opinion, it is also important to appreciate the diversity of views. The proliferation of academic and policy-focused research on this topic has brought this to the fore.

In 1982 the Prison Reform Trust (a penal pressure group) conducted the first opinion poll on crime (Shaw, 1982). Since then there has been a rapid growth of interest in public opinion, and there is now an extensive body of academic research on public perceptions of crime and criminal justice (for a detailed but accessible overview, see Roberts and Hough, 2005) alongside a prolific amount of research conducted at a local and national level by criminal justice organisations and government departments. The Crime Survey for England and Wales (formerly, the British Crime Survey) continues to be the most comprehensive and methodologically sound overview of public perceptions and the factors that influence them. In addition to contributing to academic understanding of public perceptions, this survey provides data to assess the success of criminal justice agencies in achieving targets relating to public confidence, which New Labour included in their Public Service Agreements (that is, the short- to medium-term aims and objectives of government departments specified in Comprehensive Spending Reviews). Arguably, responsiveness to public opinion became a further manifestation of managerialism (explored further in the next chapter).

At a more local level, criminal justice organisations have attempted to take stock of public opinion in the geographical areas for which they have responsibility. For example, a number of police authorities have conducted their own surveys of public perceptions of policing to gather information on the attitudes of the public to what the police are doing and should be doing, but also levels of confidence in policing. This is highly significant because confidence levels will influence the willingness of the public to report crime and to pass on information (or 'intelligence' in police discourse). In this instance, it is important to appreciate that policing is often reactive – despite attempts to adopt a more proactive stance – and the public play a pivotal role in bringing crime (and potentially offenders) to the attention of the police. This has fuelled the development of neighbourhood policing to foster closer relationships between the police (often using police community support officers) and residents and business in local communities (see Hughes and Rowe, 2007). Informal discussions with the public at this level are helpful in gauging the perceptions of policing in a neighbourhood, yet at the same time we should be mindful once more to consider whose voice gets heard. Such developments have taken place against a backdrop of political attempts to re-engage the public that extend far beyond crime policy, and these are discussed in the next chapter.

The available research recognises that a wide range of factors shape public perceptions of these phenomena (for an overview, see Wood and Viki, 2004), including direct and indirect experiences of crime and criminal justice, sociodemographic characteristics and ideological beliefs. However, there is often a lack of consensus with recent research challenging accepted wisdom. For example, van de Walle (2009) has recently used British Crime

Survey data to counter the view that citizens' experiences with the courts is related to levels of confidence, and Bradford (2011) analysed the same dataset to argue that sociodemographic factors such as age and ethnicity are not strongly linked to levels of confidence in the police.

There is insufficient space to explore this here, and instead we should note the implications of this for policy-making. In so doing, we need to appreciate the context in which public opinion is sought. The increased politicisation of law and order, discussed in the introductory chapter, is influential here. Responsiveness to public opinion is not in itself problematic, although it does raise difficulties, particularly at a more local level, if the public are invited to make recommendations for change and this is not realised in practice. It becomes problematic if the public are not well informed about crime and responses to it, and when public opinion is over-simplified and misread. The media, which we discuss in the next section, plays a dual role in terms of (mis)representing crime and justice, but also acting as a voice of the public, encouraging politicians to respond to their concerns about crime. This creates space for politicians to garner popular support for 'tough' law and order policies.

The role of the media

The media is dominant in shaping understanding of crime and criminal justice. We live in a 'fundamentally mediatised era' (Greer, 2009: 177), and due to rapid technological advances, we are constantly exposed to different forms of media as we go about our daily lives. While in the past people may have found out about crime stories through reading their daily newspaper, listening to radio news or by watching news programmes on television, it is increasingly likely that they might found out about events through looking at websites or through social media postings. The media is central to our experience of living in a 'contracted' world, with rapid exposure to crime events taking place in other countries. For example, at the time of writing, the UK media has offered extensive coverage of the trial of Anders Behring Breivik who killed 77 people in Norway in 2011. The way we access the media may well have changed, but it remains the case that the media plays a key role in the crime policy-making process. ***Box 3.5*** identifies two campaigns in which a tabloid newspaper argued for criminal justice reform. Related to this the media can create moral panics about particular events, whipping up public concern about a specific group (the 'folk devils'), urging the public to support its call for 'something to be done'.

Box 3.5: Media campaigns

The Sun is Britain's best-selling newspaper. In September 2012, its Monday to Saturday edition achieved circulation figures of approximately 2.5 million, closely followed by the 2.1 million achieved by the newly launched *Sunday* edition (Turvill, 2012). Readership figures are, of course, higher than this as newspapers are typically read by more than one person during the course of a day. Furthermore, most are now available free of charge electronically. News International owns *The Sun*. It has always been controversial but the 'phone hacking' scandal and the subsequent inquiry by Lord Justice Leveson (see www.levesoninquiry.org.uk) has drawn attention to mechanisms used to obtain stories. Traditionally a right-wing newspaper, over the past 15 years it has supported both the Labour Party and the Conservative Party. However, as we now explore, its stance on crime control is not necessarily pro-government.

'*The Sun* says no to soft justice'

Despite backing the Conservative Party in the run-up to the 2010 General Election, *The Sun* has been highly critical of the Coalition government's approach to dealing with offenders, in particular Ken Clarke's proposals, unexpectedly announced in October 2010, to reduce the prison population by 3,000 over four years (Travis and Hirsch, 2010). It drew attention to divisions within the Conservative Party on this issue by heavily publicising Boris Johnson's (the Mayor of London) view that 'soft is the perfect way to enjoy French cheese, but not how we should approach punishing criminals' (Wilson, 2011). Recurring themes within the stories are offenders being 'let off', high rates of reoffending or breach of conditions attached to Community Orders and Licences, and money wasted on offenders (particularly prisoners) or ineffective policies. Allegedly lenient sentences issued by the courts are frequently scorned.

'Broken Britain'

Since 2007, *The Sun* has frequently run stories under the campaign 'Broken Britain'. It is used to refer to the moral and social decay in society, of which crime is one symptom, along with binge drinking, teenage pregnancy and poor parenting, and to explain crimes as diverse as disorderly or anti-social behaviour through to violent crime, including gun and knife crime. This soundbite is also used by David Cameron. He first used the term as leader of the Conservative Party and pledged to 'fix Broken Britain' in the campaign running up to the 2010 General Election. It gained further impetus following the 2011 riots when it was invoked as an explanation for what politicians often termed 'sheer' or 'mindless' criminality. The Centre for Social Justice (described earlier in this chapter on page 37) also published two reports entitled *Breakdown Britain* (2006a) and *Breakthrough Britain* (2006b). This brief overview illustrates the complex relationships that characterise policy-making, involving the media, politicians and think tanks.

The media is also influential in a less direct way in shaping our perceptions of crime and its control. It provides us with both fictional and factual stories about crime from around the world as it fulfils its dual function of informing and entertaining us, paradoxically feeding our fascination with something we fear. In so doing we are exposed to a media diet of stories of violent and sexual crime, and the most dramatic aspects of the criminal justice process such as the work of detectives and criminal trials. Such topics fulfil many of the 'news values' identified by media researchers, most recently Jewkes (2010), which are essentially criteria of 'newsworthiness' used to select stories, to decide which ones to give prominence to, and to influence what aspects of the story are included and excluded. This explains the continued dominance of crime stories within television and radio news and newspapers (for an overview of relevant research, see Greer and Reiner, 2007). Scandals, which we explore shortly, capture so much media attention precisely because they are deemed newsworthy, for example, they often involve sex and/or violence, spectacle or graphic imagery, elements of risk, and they provide scope for simplification in terms of explanations or solutions offered.

The public are, of course, not passive consumers of crime stories; rather they are individuals who actively interpret the media images to which they are exposed, arriving at their own conclusions. They do not simply take at face value what they read, hear or watch. Nonetheless, the media are undoubtedly instrumental in shaping the tendency of the public (hopefully readers of this book aside!) to over-estimate the severity of the crime problem and to under-estimate the severity of the criminal justice response. Much depends, of course, on media consumption patterns. For example, readers of 'popular' newspapers are more likely to believe crime is increasing when both recorded crime statistics and victimisation studies suggest otherwise (Parfrement-Hopkins and Green, 2010).

Responding to scandal

Scandals are too rarely explored in relation to crime policy-making, and particularly by those who wish to emphasise the dominance of rationality in the policy process. However, as Downes and Morgan (2007: 231) argue, other influences on policy 'can be utterly outpaced by events which explode in such a way that unusual responses are called for', most often by the media who, as noted above, frequently claim to speak for the public.

The word 'scandal' has multiple meanings, which becomes very apparent even after a quick trawl through dictionary definitions. At its core is the act of making public concerns about behaviour that is deemed by the vast majority to be unacceptable. Often scandals refer to acts that offend the moral sensibilities of those drawing public attention to them. A recent example of a scandal is MPs submitting claims beyond what the public would classify as reasonable reimbursement for expenses associated with their employment. In relation to acts that have the potential to influence greatly the policy process, Butler and Drakeford (2005: 5) offer a useful working definition:

> Scandals are the policy equivalent of an earthquake: they are a powerful signal that change is occurring or that pressure for change has reached unsustainable levels.

In the field of criminal justice, 'crisis' is frequently used, particularly in relation to prisons (see Cavadino and Dignan, 2007), although it is worth noting that prisons are deemed to be in a permanent state of crisis, that undermines its currency as a term to refer to matters of catastrophe. In relation to crime and its control, Downes and Morgan (2012: 198) suggest that there are four categories of scandal that 'seemingly dwarf all others in their dramatic impact on politics and policy': prison escapes, miscarriages of justice, high-profile crimes and riots. The examples given by Downes and Morgan are examples of one of two broad types of scandal identified by Drakeford and Butler (2007): those which arise from a single dramatic event and are immediately and unavoidably apparent to all those involved, and those which arise from institutions and expose not sudden and traumatic events but shed light onto practices which had, in most cases, gone on for a long time and, in some, with considerable official approval. The first two examples have been more influential in the past than now. Escapes from high-security prisons are now relatively rare, and while it would be wrong to give the impression that wrongful imprisonment does not happen, in recent years attention has focused on the failing of the police rather than of the courts. The most obvious example in this respect is the investigation into the murder of Stephen Lawrence, whose racially motivated murder in 1993 led to an inquiry that exposed institutionalised racism within the police force (Macpherson, 1999). The latter two examples on the list proffered by Downes and Morgan (2012) have been highly significant. High-profile crimes typically involved murder, extreme violence or sexual offending. Such crimes dominate media headlines when they occur. They are presented in highly personalised ways, and are either associated with the name of the victim, even when the identity of the offender is known (for example, the murder of Sarah Payne in 2000 by Roy Whiting, a convicted paedophile released from prison on licence) or by the name of the offender, focusing on their pathological nature (for example, the 'Crossbow Cannibal' who was sentenced to life imprisonment in 2010 for the murder of three sex workers). Scandals become so because they stand in stark contradiction to the expectations of the locations in which they occur (Butler and Drakeford, 2005), for instance, abuse and neglect within the home which is expected to offer respite from risk and danger in public spaces, or injustice within the courts which are expected to adhere to due process. Their iconic status is often enhanced by genuine dramatic content (Drakeford and Butler, 2007), which sustains media interest.

When scandals are reported in the media, 'revelations and allegations, denials followed by explanations' (Cavender et al, 1993) are accompanied by calls for 'something' to be done. The media is often influential in this process: it presents its own opinion, often claiming to speak for the public. It increasingly provides a platform for the public to air their views, for example, by allowing members of the public to comment on news stories presented on their websites, and allows 'primary claim makers' or moral entrepreneurs such as pressure and campaigning groups to offer their own analysis of what went wrong and what should be done. There may, of course, be a lack of consensus within and between these different groups, resulting in tension and conflict. Responses can be 'knee jerk', requiring something to be done quickly in relation to highly emotive events that might be tragic or threatening. Responding in this way can be highly symbolic, offering public reassurance that the same event will not reoccur and that it has been taken seriously. There are, however, dangers attached to this approach, not least that it provides little time to explore what happened and why, or to gather evidence on the potential effectiveness of proposed solutions. A more measured response is to call for a public inquiry. In some respects, they serve a similar role to the Royal Commissions discussed earlier in this chapter. These are undertaken by formal bodies established by government to examine in close detail a matter of public concern. A notable example relating to crime is the Macpherson Inquiry, referred to above. Inevitably, this process is a time-consuming one, leading to a lengthy process of collecting evidence and preparing a detailed report. Often these produce an extensive list of recommendations (the Macpherson report contained 70 recommendations). There is, of course, no guarantee that they will be implemented. As Downes and Morgan (2012) argue, recommendations are only followed sometimes, and those that are may not be implemented in a way that results in lasting change.

Public inquiries supplement the mechanisms that already form part of the criminal justice 'machinery' to investigate complaints, which include the Independent Police Complaints Commission and the Prisons and Probation Ombudsman. The latter also respond to deaths in custody. Too frequently these tragic events fail to attract public or media attention, which underlies the point that scandals are created. Occasionally they do, for example, the murder of Zahid Mubarek by a racist cell mate in 2000, which resulted in an official inquiry (House of Commons, 2006), or the deaths of six women prisoners in Styal over a one-year period, which led to *The Corston Report* (2007) into the criminal justice response to vulnerable women. In both instances, extra-parliamentary political groups became 'moral entrepreneurs' to ensure the events were seen as 'scandalous'.

Summary

- Understanding the policy process is vital to understanding crime control.
- The policy process is 'messy': competing, and sometimes conflicting, interests influence both its development and its implementation.
- The policy process is inherently political, but to understand fully its political nature, we need to look at politics beyond Whitehall. Multilevel policy analysis provides us with a framework to look at policy networks at a national and international level.
- The public have become increasingly influential in policy-making. Their relationship with the media is crucial, but we need to guard against over-simplistic understanding of it.
- The process of policy-making contains many rational elements that should not underestimate the role of serendipity in policy-making or how emotions become intertwined in policy-making.

Questions for discussion

- Consider a recent policy development relating to crime. What were the key influences? Can you rank them in order of importance?
- Identify a crime policy which is being proposed at present, for example, one included in a Green or White Paper. Is there evidence of dissenting views in relation to its anticipated introduction?
- Consider a high-profile scandal, for example, the August 2011 riots which we began to reflect on at the beginning of this book. What impact has the scandal had on policy-making? How did the scandal interact with the other influences considered in this chapter?
- What are the relative advantages and disadvantages of seeking public opinion of matters of policy through opinion polls?

Further reading

- Drakeford, M. and Butler, I. (2007) 'Everyday tragedies: justice, scandal and young people in contemporary Britain', *The Howard Journal of Criminal Justice*, 46(3): 219–35. This article represents one of the few attempts to explore the role of scandal in crime policy-making.
- Downes, D. and Morgan, R. (2007) 'No turning back: the politics of law and order into the millennium', in M. Maguire, R. Morgan and R. Reiner (eds) *The Oxford handbook of criminology* (4th edn), Oxford: Oxford University Press. Downes and Morgan have co-authored a chapter in all five editions of *The Oxford handbook of criminology*. This version provides the greatest level of detail on the policy process.
- Hudson, J. and Lowe, S. (2009) *Understanding the policy process: Analysing welfare policy and practice*, Bristol: The Policy Press. This volume explains how and why social policy change occurs, and introduces the core concepts in policy analysis.
- Pratt, J. (2007) *Penal populism*, London: Routledge. This short volume focuses on the role of populism in penal policy-making, and considers the relationship between the politicians and those who claim to speak for the public.

Guide to electronic resources

- The official website of the **Prime Minister's Office** is www.number10.gov.uk. It is a useful resource for finding out about policy announcements (for example, via press releases, speeches and policy statements) and also about policy debates (for example, through Prime Minister's questions). You can follow Number 10 through social media and an iPhone app.
- The **Crime Survey for England and Wales** routinely collects data on public perceptions of crime and criminal justice. More detail about the survey and links to publications can be found at www.homeoffice.gov.uk/science-research/research-statistics/crime/crime-statistics/british-crime-survey
- *The Guardian* maintains a list of what it describes as Britain's most influential think tanks: www.guardian.co.uk/politics/page/2007/dec/20/1. At the time of writing, the list of 18 includes a number that have been influential in the development of crime policy, particularly in relation to drug policy (see Chapter Six), and promoting the privatisation of criminal justice functions (see Chapter Four).
- The website for the **UK Parliament** is: www.parliament.uk. It contains details of parliamentary business and provides an easy way to keep progress of current Bills. It is also possible to sign up to keep track of developments through social media.

four

Delivering crime policy: analysing the changing political landscape

Overview

In the previous chapter we explored the diverse influences that shape policy-making. This chapter focuses on the delivery of policies, but it is worth emphasising once more the absence of any unambiguous distinction between policy development and implementation. The key players involved in policy delivery are also those that also shape the policy agenda. For example, voluntary and community (or 'third') sector organisations who, as noted in the previous chapter, often combine service provision with campaigning for policy change.

Influences on the delivery of crime policies are many and varied, ranging from very practical but crucial considerations relating to resources, financial or human, through to the degree of support (or opposition) which policies receive from the public, the media, senior managers in criminal justice agencies and the professional associations which represent them, 'street-level bureaucrats' and their trade unions and pressure and campaigning groups. Rather than attempt – somewhat foolishly – to cover them all, in this chapter we pay particular attention to the rapidly changing landscape that forms the backdrop to the delivery of crime policies. This is characterised by increased partnership working and greater private and voluntary alongside more diverse public sector involvement. In so doing we explore the impact of policy agendas whose reach is far greater than crime policy, for example, the promotion of the 'Big Society', localism and decentralisation. Consequently, this chapter focuses on delivery structures rather than offering a micro-level analysis of policy in action. In so doing, it is important not to gloss over the significance of individuals and groups who operate at the 'coalface' (see page 28). Lipsky's claim (1980) that 'street-level bureaucrats' remake policies by interpreting and applying them is as relevant today as 30 years ago. 'Street-level bureaucrats' in this context are not simply the 'usual suspects' who work within criminal justice agencies such as police officers or magistrates but a wider range of individuals working within areas such as education, health and housing who could be employed by the public, private or the voluntary sector. The diversity of actors involved in crime control is one manifestation of public service reform, to which we now turn.

Key concepts
Big Society, Big/Small Government, contestability, decentralisation, joined-up government, localism, managerialism, marketisation, modernisation, partnership working, public sector reform, privatisation, street-level bureaucrats, voluntary and community sector

Managerialism, modernisation and crime control: from Thatcher through to Cameron

From 1979 onwards (and heed here the warning on page 4 about the dangers of attaching too much significance to particular dates when attempting to make sense of the past), NPM principles (see page 28), initially associated with the private sector, were transferred across to a wide range of public services (Clarke et al, 1994), which were largely seen as inefficient and unaccountable. There is now an extensive cross-disciplinary literature on managerialism that reflects on these developments, to which criminologists and social policy academics have contributed (see, for example, Clarke and Newman, 1997; Raine and Willson, 1993; Senior et al, 2007). A useful aide-memoire, albeit one that crudely characterises NPM principles, is the 3 'E's': economy, effectiveness and efficiency. When applied to the work of public sector organisations, the embodiment of NPM principles requires them to prove not only that their work produces the intended 'results', but that it is also delivered in the most cost-effective manner. 'Results' in this context is focused on outputs as a measure of productivity, for example, the time taken for a case to reach court. These, however, are not necessarily measures of success since rushing through cases could threaten due process. Targets can improve productivity but also create perverse incentives such that the 'focus on purpose [is] eclipsed by the consideration of process' (Raine and Willson, 1997: 82).

McLaughlin (2006: 241) offers a more developed definition of managerialism:

> A set of governmental knowledges, techniques and practices which aim to fracture and realign relations of power within

the core agencies of the criminal justice system in order to transform the structures and reorganize in a cost-effective manner the processes of both funding, delivering and imagining criminal justice.

This definition is useful in that it does not reduce NPM to a list of ways in which it is typically operationalised, which include league tables and key performance targets. Instead, it relates this approach to public sector reform to broader political ideologies through an analysis of power. McLaughlin's definition also emphasises the way in which public sector organisations were required to change in response to the introduction of NPM principles. Rather than simply being asked to demonstrate how effective their existing practices were, organisations were expected to undergo structural and cultural change. Central to this was the promotion of standardisation in policies and practices, which substantially reduced the autonomy of local organisations and the discretion of 'street-level bureaucrats' who worked within them. If we take one aspect of criminal justice – probation (see **Table 4.1**) – as an illustrative example, we can see unambiguous evidence of how NPM principles can fundamentally change the value base, orientation and ways of working within an organisation.

Criminal justice was no exception to the introduction of NPM principles, but developments here were slower than other social policy areas for two reasons: first, the political priority attached to law and order by the new Conservative government (see Chapter Two), and second, the positioning of criminal justice agencies away from the mainstream of public administration (Raine and Willson, 1997). However, by the mid-1980s NPM principles were evident within the majority of government-led criminal justice developments (Lacey, 1994a).

The brief discussion above hints at the ways in which 'street-level bureaucrats' may resist 'top-down' policy developments, particularly those that appear to threaten the professional values they attach significance to, for example, local autonomy and discretion. Empirical studies have explored how policies have been translated into practice. For example, Wincup's (2002) research with staff working in approved premises found that *national standards* were interpreted liberally to fit with staff expectations of the purpose of approved premises.

For the most up-to-date account of the history of probation, Mair and Burke (2011) is recommended.

Table 4.1: Modernising probation: key milestones

1984	Publication of *Statement of national objectives and priorities* (Home Office, 1984), a controversial document which aimed to encourage a degree of uniformity and consistency in order to improve performance and enhance accountability (see Wincup, 2002)
1988	*National standards* were published, first for Community Service Orders (now referred to as Community Orders with a condition of unpaid work) and four years later, for all aspects of probation practice (Home Office, 1988, 1992). Again these proved to be controversial, with Cavadino et al (1999: 104) arguing that they comprised one 'nail in the coffin of local autonomy and a further centralisation of policy-making power'
2001	Creation of a (centralised) *national* Probation Service, headed up by a director with managerial oversight of 42 areas (reduced from 54)
2004	Creation of the National Offender Management Service, which brings together the Prison and Probation Services (see www.justice.gov.uk/about/noms)
2007	Publication of the Offender Management Act 2007 which empowered the Secretary of State to commission services directly, including from private and voluntary sector providers, thus introducing contestability
2010	Reconstitution of the 42 probation areas as 'trusts', responsible for both service provision and commissioning
2012	The consultation paper *Punishment and reform: Effective Probation Service* (Ministry of Justice, 2012c) proposed that probation trusts should provide advice to the courts (in the form of pre-sentence reports); undertake risk assessments; take enforcement action when offenders breach the terms of their Community Order or post-release Licence; and supervise high-risk (mostly in terms of risk of harm) offenders. It was also suggested that trusts commission external organisations to fulfil the remaining probation functions, with the exception of a small number of areas (for example, electronic monitoring) that would be commissioned nationally.
2013	Early in 2013, the Justice Secretary (Chris Grayling) announced plans to scale back the public probation service to a core role of focusing on the most dangerous and high-risk offenders. Private and voluntary sector organisations would be commissioned to take over the majority of work with offenders by 2015 on a payment-by-results basis.

A 'New Right' Conservative government initially introduced NPM. A number of aspects of NPM mesh closely with the desire to move away from the state being a 'provider' of public services to a 'purchaser' of services offered by a free market on a competitive basis. These include requiring organisations to identify their core competencies (in other words, what they do best), costing and market testing all activities and contracting out non-essential (or 'marginal') responsibilities, for example, facilities management. The introduction of NPM within criminal justice had an instrumental orientation: to justify increased spending on law and order at a time of retrenchment elsewhere (McLaughlin et al, 2001). However, while one way of conceptualising public sector reform is to see it as a relatively autonomous process, a more plausible approach is to recognise the connection with the previous Conservative governments' desire to promote a mixed economy of provision as part of its commitment to neoliberalism. In the context of criminal justice, this approach proved controversial. Shifting the power to punish to a for-profit organisation is qualitatively different from promoting private sector involvement in fields such as health, housing or education, opening up issues about legitimacy (Sparks, 2001; Cavadino and Dignan, 2007).

While it is important to emphasise the connections between political ideology and NPM, it is equally important not to lose sight of how New Labour continued the project of public sector reform when it came to power in 1997. As McLaughlin et al (2001: 305) note, there were very clear indications before the 1997 General Election campaign that 'there would be no possibility of a return to "the golden age" of pre-managerial criminal justice'. In office, NPM was 'warmly embraced' by New Labour, and under the rubric of modernisation, was 'institutionalized and normalized' (McLaughlin et al, 2001: 313). Modernisation in this instance refers not to a series of broadbrush social developments, but as a government strategy or mode of governance (Senior et al, 2007). This is ample evidence to support McLaughlin et al's (2001: 306) claim that 'New Labour's managerial project goes wider and deeper'.

For Senior et al (2007), there are three distinctive features of New Labour's modernisation project (note that their analysis is largely reflecting on New Labour under the leadership of Tony Blair). The first is 'pluralisation'. This involves rethinking what is required to deliver a service. Traditionally, this has been a generic professional such as a police officer who has received considerable training, but that accepted wisdom has been challenged. In recent years, across criminal justice agencies new roles have been developed in which 'semi-professionals' undertake the more routine aspects of the role to 'free up' time (with potential financial savings) for professionals to concentrate on the more demanding tasks. This is seen most obviously in relation to policing, and particularly through the appointment of police community support officers whose work is largely confined to the visible acts of street patrol (see Crawford et al, 2005). These fulfil an important role in terms of public reassurance, but street patrol is time-consuming and does not always lead to tangible 'results'. The second is 'joined-up justice', which we explore in the next section. The final one is 'responsibilisation', which involves the transfer of state responsibilities to the market, comprising of voluntary and private sector organisations, alongside promoting citizen involvement. Again, we return to these issues later in the chapter. Space precludes a detailed discussion of New Labour's modernisation project, but see Senior et al (2007) for a detailed overview and McLaughlin et al (2001) for a shorter introduction that focuses on developments in crime reduction and youth justice.

The Coalition government has embraced some aspects of New Labour's modernisation agenda while quickly distancing itself from others. The Coalition government was quick to detach itself from being an over-controlling state with power heavily concentrated within Whitehall through measures such as abandoning the use of Public Service Agreements (defined on page 47), removing the Offices for Government across the nine English regions and Wales introduced in 1998, and disbanding the Audit Commission (a national body with responsibility for auditing local public services in England) in the 'bonfire of the quangos' (see Chapter Three, page 34). Simultaneously, the Coalition moved quickly to widen the purchaser–provider split through putting out to tender a far greater range of services typically provided by the state than New Labour. This was driven in part by global recession, to which one solution at a national level is to curb public spending. In Ken Clarke's speech to the Centre for Crime and Justice Studies, just over a month after becoming Justice Secretary (Clarke, 2010), he made repeated references to the acute financial crisis and the importance of developing cost-effective solutions, although he was keen to dismiss the view that policy should be determined solely by the need to reduce public spending. The unprecedented scale of the planned budget savings runs the risk of exacerbating some of the problems facing the criminal justice system and undermining some of the achievements New Labour made. These include a reduction in the level of 'volume' crime such as burglary, safer communities and more decent prisons (although there is still scope for considerable improvement) and greater levels of consideration and support for victims (see Faulkner, 2011). At the same time, they also have the potential to force policy-makers to consider more radical changes to the ways in which crime is controlled. In the same speech referred to above, Ken Clarke warned about the dangers of 'salami slicing' budgets, and advocated the need to go back to 'first principles': punishing offenders, protecting the public and providing access to justice. It is too early to comment on whether criminal justice agencies have been able to rise to the challenge of 'doing more for less'. Certainly, some of the key problems facing the criminal justice system have continued. The prison population remains high (over 85,000 at the time of writing; see Ministry of Justice, 2012d); tense relationships between the police and some communities remain, as the 2011 urban disturbances vividly illustrated (Lewis et al, 2011); and crime rates remain stubbornly high with only small year-on-year reductions (ONS, 2012).

The most obvious answer to the question of whether the need to reduce public spending or the pursuit of political ideology is driving forward reforms within criminal justice, or indeed other areas of social policy, is to reply 'both'. Financial considerations are undeniably influential but there is evidence of more ideological underpinnings with cost-based rationales being used as a 'Trojan horse' for garnering public support for reforms which might otherwise be met with resistance. Rather than being simply a pragmatic response to the current fiscal climate, the Coalition's own modernisation project is influenced heavily by a desire to promote a new form of governance, which is reflected in the White Paper *Open public services 2012*, which emphasises diversity and choice, transparency, accountability, decentralisation and value for money (HM Government, 2012).

The effectiveness of the introduction of NPM is beyond the scope of this chapter. It is often portrayed in a negative light, but this glosses over its contribution in terms of greater productivity, increased cost-efficiency and the enhanced role of consumers of criminal justice (as members of communities, victims and witnesses rather than offenders). These themes are discussed by Raine and Willson (1997), who warn against looking at the accomplishments of managerialism in its own terms without considering the consequences for the protection of human rights, reduction of crime and the promotion of due process (Raine and Willson, 1995). Below we look at partnership working, which on the face of it appears to be the most appropriate way to deliver public services through, for example, pooling resources and expertise, and coordinating work with individuals who may be accessing multiple services. However, the literature on partnership working is replete with examples of mishap and failure (Newburn, 1999), illustrating the challenges of putting this approach into practice.

Partnership working

As noted above, a distinctive aspect of New Labour's modernisation project was the promotion of 'joined-up' working. This term has multiple meanings. First, it refers to the ideal of policies being 'joined-up' at the top through the joint working of government departments, sometimes through bespoke structures. The Cabinet Office is an example of the latter. It sits at the very centre of government, supporting the development, coordination and implementation of policy across all government departments. Under New Labour, it was home to the Social Exclusion Unit, which played a pivotal role in raising awareness of the need of offenders leaving prison (see Chapter Five). Further examples of 'joined-up' working include the National Offender Management Service (see **Table 4.1**) and the Youth Justice Board, an executive non-department public body charged with strategic oversight of the youth justice system in England and Wales. Second, 'joined-up' refers to work with citizens and communities, discussed in the final section of this chapter. Third, it refers to partnership working at a local level, our main concern for the remainder of this section.

The implementation of the Crime and Disorder Act 1998 (see Chapter Two) provided the impetus for the rapid development of partnership working as a strategy of crime control. This is illustrated through the examples given in **Box 4.1**. However, in focusing on change we should not lose sight of the informal partnerships that have always existed at a local level, and there are examples of formal, but non-statutory, partnerships that predated the election of New Labour in 1997. Multi-agency bodies – Drug Action Teams – were created in England following the publication of the first strategic response to drugs in 1995 (Home Office, 1995), and Multi-agency Public Protection Panels comprising of criminal justice agencies (police, prisons, probation), in collaboration with other statutory agencies (most commonly, health, housing and social services), were already operating prior to the creation of Multi-agency Public Protection Arrangements (MAPPAs) (see **Box 4.1**) (Maguire et al, 2001). There is also a long history of partnership working in crime prevention and community safety (Liddle and Gelsthorpe, 1994; Crawford, 1998). The year 1997 is therefore a landmark in relation to the formalisation of partnership structures rather than the introduction of collaborative working.

Box 4.1: Examples of partnership working

The partnerships listed below are all examples of what Carnwell and Carson (2005: 9) refer to as 'problem-oriented' partnerships. They are premised on the belief that the 'traditional' approach to tackling the 'problem' was ineffective and that a partnership response offers a more effective solution. They all operate, albeit to varying extents, on what might be termed a 'macroscopic' (strategic) and a 'mediscopic' (operational) level (see Carnwell and Buchanan, 2005a: 267).

- **Community Safety (or Crime and Disorder Reduction) Partnerships** were created through the Crime and Disorder Act 1998 to develop and implement strategies to protect local communities from crime and reduce fear of crime. There are currently 310 such partnerships in England and a further 22 in Wales.
- **Multi-agency Public Protection Arrangements (MAPPAs):** the current structures (located in each of the 42 criminal justice areas) were established

by the Criminal Justice and Court Services Act 2000. They are tasked with managing the risk posed by registered sex offenders, violent and other types of sexual offenders, and offenders who pose a serious risk of harm to the public.

- **Youth Offending Teams:** established following the Crime and Disorder Act 1998 in each of the 157 local authorities in England and Wales with responsibility for preventing (re)offending by children and young people aged between 10 and 17.

The precise membership of the partnerships listed above varies, but all involve criminal agencies working in partnership with other statutory agencies, for example, relating to health, education, employment, housing, and children and young people's services.

There is now a vast literature on partnership working, some of which is practically oriented, for example, evaluations of how these structures operate in practice (see, for example, Duke and MacGregor, 1997 on Drug Action Teams; Kemshall and Hilder, 2012 on MAPPAs; and Souhami, 2007, on Youth Offending Teams), while other writings try to locate partnership working in its sociopolitical context and look at this approach theoretically (see Carnwell and Carson, 2005). The available literature points to a series of problems with partnership working, which demonstrate that partnership is a means to an end, not an end in itself, and that new arrangements have to become embedded within a context in which each organisation has its own culture or indeed cultures (see, for example, Mawby and Worrall's recent work on cultures within probation, 2011).

Within the literature the recurrent difficulties identified include communication problems, battles over 'territory' and resources, differences of power between agencies, especially between small and large organisations, clashing philosophies and confusion about roles and responsibilities (see Carnwell and Buchanan, 2005b). Listing the difficulties has allowed researchers to 'read off' the essential attributes of effective partnerships. They are helpfully summarised by Carnwell and Carson (2005: 8) as trust, respect for partners, joint working, teamwork, eliminating boundaries and being an ally. While useful, this creates the impression that partnership work needs to be refined further in order to be effective in a manner that glosses over the wider sociopolitical context in which they operate. Crawford (1998), reflecting predominantly on partnerships operating within the community safety sphere, questions the compatibility between NPM and the establishment of genuine partnerships based on trust and cooperation because they run the risk of promoting insularity and competition rather than reciprocity and interdependence.

The rapid promotion of partnership working provides evidence of the emergence of new forms of governance. For Parrott (2005), New Labour's approach was to maintain consistency in partnership working across the UK through mechanisms such as audits and contracts, while devolving as much operational power as possible to the partnership organisations. Thus the partnership agenda was not simply about being more economic, effective and efficient, but formed part of a broader modernisation project. The creation of a myriad of partnerships, which could then be managed centrally, would ultimately allow the government to become an enabler, steering rather than rowing (see Braithwaite, 2000). All the partnerships listed in **Box 4.1** have responsibility for managing budgets and commissioning services, although the role of Community Safety Partnerships will be transformed once Police and Crime Commissioners take up their positions in each of the 43 police forces in England and Wales (for a critical discussion of their role, see Morgan, 2013). Elections for these posts, which will replace the current system of police authorities, took place in November 2012. There have already been concerns raised about the ability of these individuals to work in partnership with local organisations that might have differing views on how best to tackle crime (Collins, 2012).

Reflecting on who is involved in partnership structures, it becomes apparent that there is relatively little private sector involvement, particularly in contrast to voluntary sector involvement, whose role in the newest partnership structure – Integrated Offender Management (see **Box 4.2**) – is being actively promoted by the Home Office in collaboration with Clinks (described on page 36) (Home Office, 2012a). MAPPA is an exception here. Since the Criminal Justice Act 2003, members of the public – known as lay advisers – form part of the Strategic Management Boards that have oversight of the MAPPA in each area. They can be classed as users in the sense that they form part of the community that the MAPPA is expected to protect from harm. Some also include representatives of the private sector when they operate prisons in the area and electronic monitoring. Focusing on developments in the community safety arena, Crawford (1998) comments on limited private sector involvement despite being encouraged explicitly through government policy statements since 1984. He attributes the lack of participation to the difficulties of persuading profit-maximising businesses that it is in their best interests (in an economic sense) to participate. This is likely to change as crime control becomes further marketised, opening up opportunities from which the private sector is most likely to benefit.

Box 4.2: Integrated Offender Management

Integrated Offender Management is also a 'problem-oriented' partnership, which operates at a 'mediscopic' (operational) level (see page 62 for a discussion of this term) to reduce reoffending among the most prolific offenders. Piloted initially in six sites (see Senior et al, 2011), it is an example of a co-located service, involving professionals from different agencies and sectors being physically located within the same building, sharing a caseload of offenders. The aim was for professionals from each agency to work together to provide an end-to-end approach to offenders in need of intense management. The concept of Integrated Offender Management builds on existing partnership arrangements for prolific offenders, as well as those targeted at drug users such as the Drug Interventions Programme (see *Box 6.3*). The process evaluation (Senior et al, 2011) shed light on joined-up working. It found strong evidence that co-locating professionals helped to resolve competing agendas, but noted too that operational leadership was contested at some sites between police and probation, and not all sites had managed to secure the involvement of a wider range of partners, for example, prisons, Youth Offending Teams and the voluntary and community sector.

Marketising crime control

As we have already explored, the Coalition embraced the desire to promote a mixed economy of provision within crime control that had been set in motion by previous governments. Its *Programme for government* promised a 'rehabilitation revolution' that would 'pay independent providers to reduce reoffending, paid for by the savings this new approach will generate within the criminal justice system' (HM Government, 2010a). This was previously included in the Conservative but not the Liberal Democrat manifesto. A potential advantage of the new funding mechanisms, which we explore shortly, is attracting new market entrants in the hope that it will lead to innovative and creative practice and the fostering of skills and expertise (see Ministry of Justice, 2010). Theoretically these new entrants might come from any sector. However, as we discuss in the next section, the voluntary sector may be disadvantaged when bidding against commercial organisations, who can now draw on considerable expertise of working with offenders, as described in *Box 4.3*.

> **Box 4.3:** Examples of private sector involvement in crime control
>
> - **Court escort services for prisoners:** this important but ancillary function was the first aspect of imprisonment to be privatised in 1993, paving the way for greater private sector involvement in building and managing prisons.
> - **Electronic monitoring:** since it was first used for defendants on bail in 1989 (see Mair and Nee, 1990), the private sector has had sole responsibility for this aspect of crime control, which is now used to monitor offenders subject to curfew requirements attached to their Community Orders and Suspended Sentence Orders or for short- to medium-term prisoners released from prison in advance of their release date (Nellis and Mair, 2012).
> - **Imprisonment:** the UK has the most privatised prison system in Europe, with 14 per cent of the total prisoner population housed in private prisons (Prison Reform Trust, 2013).
> - **Police custody suites:** a number of police forces already use private sector companies to manage custody suites, justified in terms of freeing up police time to focus on core functions. Private sector companies provide a range of professionals including healthcare and forensic professionals. This development can also be viewed against the backdrop of the rise of 'semi-professionalisation' across the police service (discussed on page 59).
> - **Regulation and security** (typically of private commercial space such as shopping centres): 'policing' is no longer synonymous with the (public) 'police' and there is substantial evidence of a pluralisation of policing involving an increasingly complex array of public, private and municipal bodies in the provision of regulation and security (Jones and Newburn, 1996; Crawford et al, 2005).

Developed further in the Green Paper *Breaking the cycle: Effective punishment, rehabilitation and the sentencing of offenders* (Ministry of Justice, 2010), the 'rehabilitation revolution' refers to new approaches of working with offenders (for example, a focus on drug recovery rather than maintenance discussed in Chapter Six) and also new ways of funding and delivering services through the introduction of PbR. This funding mechanism is not peculiar to criminal justice and is used in other policy areas, beginning with the National Health Service in 2003/04 when payments were linked to the number and type of patients treated (Fox and Albertson, 2011). In 2011, the Department for Work and Pensions introduced this mechanism in relation to its Work Programme (see **Box 5.3**). PbR allows the government to purchase services on the basis that the provider will be paid according to the outcomes achieved rather than the inputs or outputs. For example, rather than requiring organisations working with offenders to hit targets in relation to the numbers who enrol on a particular programme or the number who enter employment, education or training, they are required to demonstrate that their intervention has had a positive impact on rates of reoffending. The cost of the service will be funded through reductions in costs to the state if fewer people reoffend. The expectation is that a greater focus on outcomes will lead to more economic, efficient and innovative ways of working, particularly against a backdrop of increasing competition among potential providers (see the Ministry of Justice's *Competition strategy for offender services*, 2011a).

The extent to which this represents a departure from the past is worthy of speculation. New Labour was committed to modernising the public sector (in relation to criminal justice, see Senior et al, 2007) but has been accused by the Coalition government of being top-down and prescriptive (described as a 'Whitehall knows best' approach), and failing to focus sufficiently on the achievement of results because it was pre-occupied with targets (Ministry of Justice, 2010: 6). Evidently the reforms will 'accelerate the growth of a social investment market' (Whitfield, 2012: 22) in the sphere of criminal justice, and radically alter the role and size of the state as some of the crime control functions it has previously fulfilled directly are transferred to other providers, creating a 'mixed economy'. In essence, state functions will be 'hollowed out' and the state will become a 'market creator' (Gough, 2012: 20). Arguably, what lies ahead is more akin to a funding rather than rehabilitation revolution, particularly when reforms take place against a backdrop of a rising prison population and a shared commitment to punitiveness across the political spectrum (Gough, 2012).

For governments, PbR is attractive in that it appears to effectively transfer risk and responsibility to those who have invested in the project, although as Whitfield (2012) suggests, it is far from risk-free. The investor may be the independent provider, but the delay between providing the service and receiving payment can be lengthy, so alternative funding may be needed to meet the initial costs. Whether the reforms are motivated by the economic crisis or are ideologically driven is a moot point. Certainly, it has been suggested that criminal justice reforms are less about reducing the financial deficit and instead about the pursuit of a 'profoundly ideological project, intent on shrinking state provision into an ephemeral "Big Society" ragbag of provisions' (Silvestri, 2011: 3). This is refuted by the Coalition government who instead emphasise more pragmatic reasons for engaging a wider range of players in terms of capitalising on the different strengths of organisations who might contribute to the rehabilitation process (Rodger, 2012).

Enter the 'Big Society'

The 'Big Society' gained momentum in political discourse in the 2010 General Election campaign. The concept refers to 'a society with much higher levels of personal, professional, civic and corporate responsibility' (Conservative Party, 2010). It owes its origins to the influence of think tanks (see Bochel, 2011). It can be argued that the strength of the concept – the breadth of its vision – is also its core weakness in that it is difficult to articulate to the public (and crucially voters) what it means in practice and what is required to mend a 'broken society' (see page 49) characterised by, for example, family breakdown, welfare dependency and crime. To those with an interest in the changing form of governance its message was far clearer: it represented a shift away from 'Big Government' through the transfer of responsibilities from the central state to civil society, which includes voluntary and community sector organisations, social enterprises and the private sector (see Bochel, 2011). This agenda is embraced in the Localism Act 2011 that aims to shift power from central government, not simply to local government but also to individuals and communities. The preamble to the Act obfuscates its key intentions to 'responsibilise' individuals and communities and to promote 'Smaller Government'. This sits somewhat awkwardly, as Hough (2011: 218) suggests, with crime policy, because it is an area where the government tends to make bold claims that it exercises 'tight control over the levers for crime reduction'. We concentrate in this section on the promotion of voluntary and community sector organisations, mindful that behind the notion of the 'Big Society' lurks the 'Big Market' (Morgan, 2012). Readers are also referred back to earlier discussions of the creation of Police and Crime Commissioners and new mechanisms used to promote public input into the shaping of public services (see pages 64 and 45-8 respectively), alongside the Coalition government's agenda to promote opportunities for citizens to 'take part' described at the end of this chapter in the 'Guide to electronic resources' section.

In a piece reflecting on crime and justice in the 'Big Society', Morgan (2012) questions whether it offers more than 'old wine in new bottles'. This appears to be a legitimate question to ask in relation to voluntary and community sector involvement. The New Labour governments put in place strategic measures to enhance the role of the voluntary sector. They engaged in capacity-building initiatives, channelled through the Office of the Third Sector. Their willingness to embrace the voluntary and community sector was closely related to their stated commitment to renew the institutions and processes of civil society and to promote active citizenship through, among other things, greater levels of volunteering. In 2008, the Ministry of Justice set out its strategy to enhance the role of the voluntary sector (which is heavily reliant, but not exclusively, on volunteers) in campaigning, strengthening communities, transforming public services and encouraging social enterprise (Ministry of Justice, 2008). The criminal justice system shared this enthusiasm for working with the voluntary sector, and developed a complementary strategy (Ministry of Justice, 2008), which outlined how it would engage with the voluntary sector to deliver better public services and improve policy through effective partnership. It also set out principles for working with the voluntary sector to reduce reoffending and to protect the public.

There is a long-established tradition of using the voluntary sector to provide services within the criminal justice process (Hucklesby and Worrall, 2007; Maguire, 2013), but until fairly recently input from the voluntary sector has been confined to offering supplementary services (Hucklesby and Worrall, 2007). The introduction of the Offender Management Act 2007 (see *Table 4.1*) has allowed the voluntary sector to compete to deliver core services. For example, the proliferation of mentoring, described in *Box 4.4*, has allowed voluntary sector organisations to become involved in the provision of both supplementary (for example, working with short-term prisoners) *and* core services (for example, as illustrated by its inclusion in the Integrated Offender Management project; see *Box 4.2*).

Box 4.4: Mentoring in criminal justice

Since the late 1980s, there has been a rapid growth in interest in mentoring in the UK and elsewhere, and mentoring schemes are now found in 'every corner of public policy' (Boaz and Pawson, 2005: 175) to address social issues as diverse as bullying, drug use, lone parenthood and homelessness. Despite, and perhaps because of, its widespread use there remains an extensive debate about what constitutes mentoring. As Philip and Spratt (2007: 5) note, mentoring 'holds different meanings for different participants and is used in many different ways'. There is, however, some consensus, and mentoring typically involves a one-to-one relationship between a mentor and mentee, working to clearly defined goals and within set timeframes (Mentoring and Befriending Foundation, 2012). Within the criminal justice process, mentoring is now widespread, especially in the youth justice system where it is used both as a preventative tool with individuals who have been identified as 'at risk' of offending and as a reactive tool for those who have already been charged with, or convicted of, offences (see Porteous, 2006). Mentoring schemes for adults caught up in the criminal justice process are less prevalent but are growing in number, and are currently found at all stages of the criminal justice process, particularly post-release from custody. Most recently it has been announced that mentoring should be extended to all prisoners leaving custody after serving a short sentence (BBC News, 2012). Mentoring at the pre-trial stage remains in its infancy but was included in the Effective Bail Scheme pilots.

While mentoring for offenders is currently in vogue, it is important to acknowledge that it is not a wholly new idea, and there are considerable parallels between mentoring and the 'tracking' schemes that were introduced in England for young offenders in the early 1980s (Nellis, 2004). The roots of the mentoring scheme for offenders also lie in the philanthropic tradition of encouraging community participation in assisting and supporting offenders that influenced the development of the Probation Service (see Mair and Burke, 2011).

The Coalition has continued with initiatives to promote voluntary and community sector involvement, albeit in different guises and with reduced funding (Maguire, 2012). Most notably, it reformulated the Office of the Third Sector as the Office for Civil Society only a matter of days after forming a government. On the face of it, it has also created opportunities for greater voluntary sector involvement through further marketisation. However, while the Green Paper refers directly to 'small and specialist voluntary providers' (Ministry of Justice, 2010: 41), there are genuine concerns about whether this will provide 'real' opportunities, especially for small-scale and/or highly specialist organisations (for an insightful analysis of this issue, see Maguire, 2012). For example, a small project working with young female offenders in one city would find it difficult to bid for funding without joining forces with a large voluntary sector organisation or a commercial provider. If they were unable or unwilling to do this, their relative advantages such as good working relationships with the local community or the uniqueness of their approach to resettling a particular group would be lost (see Gough, 2012: 21). While some small organisations might be willing to move from the margins, others may be fearful that this will threaten their independence as they become 'prisoners' rather than 'partners' (Silvestri, 2009). Voluntary sector organisations most likely to 'survive' in what Gough (2012: 20) terms the 'hybrid philanthro-capitalist structure' are those which are large-scale with a national base, that can mimic the business practices of private sector corporations to remain competitive, rather than smaller ones which are locally based. Consequently, as Rodger (2012: 19) argues, the introduction of PbR may prove to be antithetical to the notion of the 'Big Society', through 'colonising' the voluntary sector and promoting the 'industrialisation' of rehabilitation.

Summary

- The range of players responsible for delivering crime policy is changing. It includes organisations across the public, private and voluntary sectors, often working in partnership. However, in emphasising change we should not lose sight of the fact that cross-sector involvement has always characterised the delivery of crime policy.
- Partnership working has the potential to offer more effective ways of working but is not a 'silver bullet'.
- Marketisation can be described as a 'juggernaut' (to borrow Giddens' 1990 metaphor for the modern world). This approach is being deployed at a rapid pace across different crime policy spheres with little reflection on the consequences of this approach for the delivery of crime policies or consideration of alternative strategies.
- The 'Big Society' offers the potential for radical and large-scale change. While speculating on the future might be considered a dangerous pastime (as we note in the concluding chapter), greater private sector involvement in crime control appears to be the most likely outcome in the short term.

Questions for discussion

- Select one policy area (possibly one of those included in Chapters Five, Six and Seven) and identify the key players in delivering policies 'on the ground'. Note the potential benefits of a partnership approach and possible areas of conflict.
- How can we account for the enhanced role of the private sector in delivery of criminal justice?
- What are the relative advantages and disadvantages of voluntary sector involvement in controlling crime?
- Should the public play a greater role in controlling crime? Conduct a SWOT analysis (strengths, weaknesses, opportunities and threats) to help you formulate your argument.

Further reading

- Carnwell, R. and Buchanan, J. (2008) *Effective practice in health, social care and criminal justice* (2nd edn), Buckingham: Open University Press. This edited collection explores the context in which multi-agency partnerships have developed and operate, their practical applications to a range of 'problems' including drug use and domestic violence, and lessons learned from partnership working.
- Faulkner, D. and Burnett, R. (2011) *Where next for criminal justice?*, Bristol: The Policy Press. This ambitious book reviews government policies, identifying the lessons that can be learned. It draws on academic research and also Faulkner's extensive experience as a senior civil servant at the Home Office.

- Hough. M., Allen, R. and Padel, U. (eds) (2006) *Reshaping probation and prisons: The new Offender Management Framework*, Bristol: The Policy Press. This slim edited collection contains six essays by leading criminologists who reflect critically on proposals to transform the structures for working with offenders.
- Lipsky, M. (2010) *Street-level bureaucracy: Dilemmas of the individual in public services* (updated edn), New York: Russell Sage Foundation. This book provides an insight into the critical role played by those who implement policies across a range of public services, including law enforcement.

Guide to electronic resources

- **Clinks** is described on page 36. From www.clinks.org you can follow the links to websites of a wide range of voluntary sector organisations that work with offenders.
- The official website of the **Prime Minister's Office** (see page 54) is www.number10. gov.uk. It includes a drop-down menu entitled 'Take Part' which details under six headings (your neighbourhood, public engagement, giving [both time and money], community safety and recognising others) 26 different ways in which members of the public can do so. Those most relevant to controlling crime are attending police beat meetings, becoming a special constable and joining Neighbourhood Watch.
- Information on **community safety partnerships** can be found on the Home Office website: www.homeoffice.gov.uk/crime/partnerships/
- The **Adam Smith Institute** (www.adamsmith.org) is a think tank whose stated aims are to promote libertarian and free market ideas through research, publishing and media commentary. It runs an educational programme specifically directed at students. It is well known for its work on privatisation (including prisons) and public sector reform. From time to time, crime is referred to in its blog (use the search function to locate relevant discussions).

The resettlement of prisoners: back on the policy agenda

Overview

Resettlement is now high on the policy agenda of England and Wales, and over the past 15 years there has been a proliferation of new resettlement initiatives working with prisoners, one of the most socially excluded groups of society. Projects often target short-sentence prisoners (those serving sentences under 12 months) who are not subject to supervision by the Probation Service on release. Resettlement projects typically attempt to reduce high rates of reoffending among prisoners. The voluntary sector is a key player in these initiatives, but private sector involvement is likely to increase substantially in the future as the Coalition government embarks on its 'rehabilitation revolution'. This chapter uses resettlement as a case study to explore the wider policy issues that have been introduced in earlier chapters. They include the impact of marketisation, the role of evidence in policy-making and the relationship between social and crime policies.

Key concepts
Evidence-based policy, imprisonment, marketisation, PbR (Payment by Results), rehabilitation revolution, reoffending, social exclusion

The resettlement of prisoners

Between April 2011 and March 2012, 86,391 adults (that is, those aged 21 and over) were released from prisons in England and Wales after serving determinate sentences, of which just over half (54 per cent) served sentences of less than 12 months (Ministry of Justice, 2012a). A likely outcome is that they will be reconvicted for another offence, sometimes resulting in a further prison sentence. Figures for 2010 reveal that almost half (48 per cent) were reconvicted of an offence committed within one year of leaving custody, with former prisoners committing an average of four offences (Ministry of Justice, 2012a). High reconviction rates are, in part, a consequence of the multiple and complex problems faced by this group which range from substantive issues such as homelessness or unemployment through to less tangible ones relating to relationships and attitudes (see Social Exclusion Unit, 2002). A further likely outcome is that those released on either Home Detention Curfew or Licence will be returned to custody for failing to keep to the terms on which their release was conditional. Recalls to custody have risen sharply since the turn of the 21st century, and on 30 September 2012 those recalled to prison made up 6 per cent of the prison population (Ministry of Justice, 2012a). For this reason, Padfield and Maruna (2006) suggest the 'prison gate' for many is in practice a 'revolving door'.

Both the policies and practices of prisoner resettlement has been the subject of considerable research over the past decade (for a useful collection which brings together the writings of many experts in this area, see Hucklesby and Hagley-Dickinson, 2007a). In this chapter we focus on three aspects and use the resettlement of prisoners to illustrate some of the broader policy issues introduced in earlier chapters. These are, first, the changing landscape of how resettlement services are delivered and funded; second, the extent to which developments relating to resettlement policy and practice can be described as evidence based; and third, how social policy interacts with crime control policies. Before we explore these issues, we unpack the concept of resettlement and briefly consider why it has risen up the criminal justice policy agenda in recent years in England and Wales. While it has similarly become a significant policy issue in Scotland (see, for example, The Scottish Prisons Commission, 2008) and Northern Ireland (see, for example, Criminal Justice Inspection Northern Ireland, 2011), this is beyond the scope of this chapter.

The recent history of resettlement

As others have noted, defining resettlement 'is no easy task' (Hucklesby and Hagley-Dickinson, 2007b: 2). In the past, resettlement has been referred to as 'aftercare' and 'throughcare' (Maguire and Raynor, 1997; Maguire et al, 2000). Resettlement entered into criminal justice discourse in the late 1990s (see Home Office, 1998b), and was firmly in place when the Resettlement Pathfinders were established under the Crime Reduction Programme (see **Box 3.3**), which we explore shortly. Resettlement has become an umbrella term for a range of activities and practices with prisoners, resulting in ambiguity and misunderstanding (Raynor, 2007). Raynor (2007) observes two areas where there is little consensus: the goals of resettlement and the reasons for providing it as part of the criminal justice process. The latter opens up a debate about whether crime control agencies should address the welfare needs of prisoners.

The concept of resettlement implies that prisoners' lives were 'settled' prior to their release. It also implies that it is desirable to return offenders to their communities. However, attempting to resettle prisoners in those communities from which they originally lived may return them to lives that are essentially criminogenic. In many respects, notions of resettlement are based on implicit normative understandings of 'mainstream society' characterised by pro-social relationships, adequate resources and a good quality of life (Moore, 2012). The Home Office Resettlement Survey (Niven and Stewart, 2005) revealed that the lives of many prisoners are far removed from this. It discovered that they often experience insecure housing and unemployment, and rough sleeping and a lifetime of worklessness are not uncommon. In other countries such as the US, the concept of 'resettlement' is rarely deployed, and instead the term 're-entry' is used to describe the process (Maruna and LeBel, 2002; Petersilia, 2003). For Moore (2012), the latter term has considerable analytic advantages in that it appears more open, with less interventionist connotations. Thus it focuses on wider interactions between offenders and society as opposed to what actions state and voluntary sector agencies might take to protect the public and to reduce reoffending. This might include exclusionary practices that we consider at the end of this chapter in relation to employment and housing.

In the late 1990s a series of important policy developments relating to prisoners making the transition from prison to the community began, starting with the Resettlement Pathfinders described in *Box 5.2*. In 2001, HM Inspectorates of Prisons and Probation published a report entitled *Through the prison gate* based on a joint thematic review. It made a series of recommendations, calling for a resettlement strategy, a greater focus on short-sentence prisoners (who are not subject to probation supervision on release) and more effective working between prison and probation to offer 'through the gate' support for prisoners serving sentences lasting over one year. While the report made explicit that responsibility for resettling prisoners was the role of the criminal justice system – as part of its overall aim to prevent reoffending and to protect the public – it also drew attention to the potential role to be played by family members and community agencies, and implicitly, by supporting the use of Home Detention Curfews, the private sector who are responsible for the electronic monitoring of offenders subject to these (Dodgson et al, 2001). A year later, the Social Exclusion Unit (2002) published an influential report entitled *Reducing reoffending by ex-prisoners.* In many respects, this report illustrates vividly New Labour's 'tough on crime, tough on the causes of crime' policy agenda. Central to the report was identifying what Miliband (2005, cited in Levitas et al, 2007) has termed 'deep' social exclusion, which draws attention to the multiple, complex and interacting problems experienced by prisoners.

> Before they ever come into contact with the prison system, most prisoners have a history of social exclusion, including high levels of family, educational and health disadvantage, and poor prospects in the labour market. The failure of mainstream agencies to deal with these aspects of social exclusion means that the Prison Service and Probation Service are in many cases being asked to put right a lifetime of social exclusion. (Social Exclusion Unit, 2002: 18)

In so doing it painted a picture of the typical prisoner as unemployed and dependent on state benefits; possessing few qualifications and basic skills; in poor health, both physically and mentally; homeless or living in temporary accommodation; and with weak family ties. At the same time it noted even higher levels of social exclusion among young adult prisoners (that is, those aged 18–20), and prisoners from black and minority ethnic backgrounds who are over-represented in the penal system. Essentially the Social Exclusion Unit report – like the earlier HM Inspectorates of Prison and Probation (2001) report – identified 'deficits' within the prisoners' lives which needed to be 'fixed' in order to reduce both the quantifiable financial costs associated with frequent known reoffending by former prisoners and direct and indirect victimisation (the latter referring to their families and their communities) and the social costs for offenders and their families. It made a series of recommendations, including a 'National Rehabilitation Strategy' (Social Exclusion Unit, 2002).

In response to the recommendations of both these reports (HM Inspectorates of Prisons and Probation, 2001; Social Exclusion Unit, 2002), the Home Office published *Reducing reoffending: National action plan* in 2004. Comprising of seven pathways (accommodation; education, training and employment; mental and physical health; drugs and alcohol; finance, benefits and debts; children and families; and attitudes and thinking), it aimed to offer a framework for reducing reoffending. For each pathway a plan of action was outlined at the national, regional and local level, identifying lead agencies (from within the criminal justice system) and a long list of partners including public sector organisations (for example, Jobcentre Plus, National Treatment Agency for Substance Misuse) and statutory partnerships (for example, Drug Action Teams, Sure Start partnerships).

The title of this strategic document made it apparent why New Labour felt that criminal justice agencies, in partnership with other key stakeholders, should address the welfare needs of prisoners. Social exclusion is mentioned only twice within the document, and in contrast, reducing reoffending appears 27 times.

In the plan it stated that the implementation of the Criminal Justice Act 2003 would be a 'key building block' (Home Office, 2004b: 3). This important piece of legislation created a new sentencing framework and made far-reaching changes to community sentences through the development of a generic Community Order which allows sentencers to choose from a 'menu' of 12 interventions and to vary the level of supervision according to the risk/need profile of offenders (that is, the nature and level of risk they are judged to pose to others and themselves and their assessed needs, particularly those believed to be related to their offending) and the nature of their offence(s) (for an introductory overview, see Worrall and Canton, 2013). It also introduced Custody Plus as a replacement for prison sentences of less than 12 months, which would combine a period in custody (between two and thirteen weeks) with probation supervision in the community (of at least six months). The intention was that all prisoners – regardless of sentence length – would be released on licence and thus would receive support 'through the prison gate'. As others have noted (Hucklesby and Hagley-Dickinson, 2007b), these proposals were largely well received, although they ran the risk of increasing the prison population if sentencers were encouraged to use this disposal for offenders who previously would have received a community penalty. Custody Plus remained 'on the books' but not implemented for almost a decade until it was abolished by the Legal Aid, Sentencing and Punishment of Offenders Act 2012.

The discussion above relates to policy developments that have focused predominantly on the majority of prisoners who are released from custody. Based on data from April 2012 to June 2012 (Ministry of Justice, 2012a), these are typically male (91 per cent) and serving sentences of less than four years (89 per cent). They are also likely to be under 40 since on 30 September 2012, over two thirds of the prison population (70 per cent) fell within this age group (Ministry of Justice, 2012a). Relatively few will be assessed as posing sufficient risk of harm to others to merit the need for MAPPAs, and thus intense supervision in the community, because these are usually put in place for sex offenders who make up a small proportion of those received into custody each year. A growing body of literature has documented the specific resettlement experiences of atypical groups of prisoners including women (Gelsthorpe and Sharpe, 2007; McIvor et al, 2009), lifers (Appleton, 2010), young prisoners (Hagell, 2004; Hazel, 2004), older prisoners (Crawley, 2004; Crawley and Sparks, 2006) and dangerous prisoners (Kemshall, 2007; Mills and Grimshaw, 2012). Developing specific projects for these groups is just one example of the rapid changing landscape of resettlement services over the past 15 years.

Delivering resettlement services: a rapidly changing landscape

Since the late 1990s, the range of organisations involved in delivering resettlement services to prisoners, both within custody and in the community, has grown rapidly. The voluntary sector, as discussed in the previous chapter, has played a key role in this respect, mirroring their enhanced role in crime control more generally. Hucklesby and Worrall (2007: 174) describe it as a 'trailblazer' for the provision of resettlement services, suggesting that it has plugged gaps in provision (for example, support for short-sentence prisoners) and built up knowledge and experience that can be shared with criminal justice agencies. Voluntary sector involvement in supporting offenders leaving custody is not new. The resettlement of offenders only became a statutory responsibility in 1862 and, prior to this, charities – often faith-based ones – were involved in supporting prisoners under the guise of 'Discharged Prisoners' Aid' (Hedderman, 2007). Even after the state assumed responsibility for the resettlement of prisoners, the voluntary sector continued to play a pivotal role, although it became more organised, secular and professional. It took particular responsibility for voluntary aftercare (with short-sentence prisoners) until 1963 when this became the responsibility of the Probation Service (Raynor, 2007). Probation's involvement in voluntary aftercare was relatively short-lived and, as Raynor (2007) notes, by the mid-1980s the Probation Service began to withdraw from this work, focusing instead on providing 'throughcare' supervision with prisoners released on statutory licence (those serving sentences greater than 12 months). This formed part of a wider development of the Probation Service moving from 'advise, assist and befriend' to 'control, confront and monitor' (Worall and Hoy, 2005).

Voluntary sector organisations now working to resettle prisoners include those who have always targeted offenders (for example, Nacro), as well as those whose core client groups have traditionally been other socially excluded individuals such as the homeless (for example, the St Giles Trust) or vulnerable young people (for example, the Depaul Trust). With relatively few exceptions (for example, the Resettlement Pathfinders, discussed in *Box 5.2*), resettlement projects have not been able to access core government funding. As a result, they have looked to other sources of funding, and successful bids often have 'strings attached'. For example, projects that have received funding from the European Social Fund have been required to support its aims to extend employment opportunities and to develop a skilled and adaptable workforce (see www.dwp.gov. uk/esf/). One example in this respect is PS Plus, described on page 82. Alternative sources of funding are also usually time-limited and this can have major ramifications for projects: it can make it hard to attract and retain high-quality staff; time is invested in securing additional funds rather than developing the project; and it is can be difficult to establish a long-term vision.

Resettlement projects proliferated in the early part of the 21st century as organisations seized the opportunity to establish links with prisons. They were keen to invest time and energy developing projects that could form the basis of a bid for government funding when Custody Plus was introduced, and the recommendations of the Carter report (2003) were translated into practice. This essentially opened up the market for statutory, voluntary and private sector organisations to offer core Offender Management functions (see Burke, 2005; Hough et al, 2006). In 2006, it was announced that its introduction had been postponed indefinitely on the grounds of insufficient resources (Sevdiren, 2011), creating uncertainty among providers of resettlement services.

On the face of it, the change of government in May 2010 created further opportunities for voluntary sector organisations to obtain contracts to provide resettlement services within prisons and the community, and the government's proposals (described in the previous chapter) have been welcomed, albeit somewhat cautiously, by the voluntary sector (see Clinks, 2011). However, there is a real risk that voluntary sector involvement might be sidelined (described in the previous chapter) as large, multinational private organisations become the preferred providers. If greater private sector involvement is realised in practice it will represent a significant departure from the past with respect to supporting prisoners. The private sector has rarely been involved in resettlement (for an exception, see Maguire et al's evaluation of the Transitional Support Scheme published in 2010 which involved G4S).

Pilot PbR projects for resettling prisoners were among the first to be developed. The HMP Peterborough Resettlement Project – described in **Box 5.1** – predates the Coalition government's drive to introduce PbR. It was set up by the New Labour government, quashing the view that the PbR approach is the 'brainchild' of the Coalition government (Fox and Albertson, 2011: 396). This project relies on Social Impact Bonds (for an introductory overview, see Whitfield, 2012), which can operate on either a commercial or philanthropic basis (Mulgan et al, 2011) to plug the 'finance gap'.

Box 5.1: Social Impact Bond pilot at HMP Peterborough

The Social Impact Bond pilot was launched in 2010 at HMP Peterborough. Social Finance (a financial intermediary established in 2007 to develop social investment) commissioned the St Giles Trust to work in partnership with other voluntary sector providers to work intensively with adult male prisoners serving sentences of less than 12 months. The project had a specific aim to encourage 'early engagement, through and beyond the gate and individualised support in the community to address needs and prevent reoffending' (St Giles Trust, 2012). In this instance, the number of court reconvictions serves as a proxy measure for reoffending (Disley et al, 2011). Known as the One Service, the project trains former offenders to become peer advisers to work with prisoners who otherwise would not receive any support in the community. Typical tasks include assisting with finding accommodation, meeting prisoners at the gate and taking them to appointments plus referring them to specialist support services. It is intended that the project will work with 3,000 prisoners over a six-year period, both while they are in custody and on release (St Giles Trust, 2012). Early reports of levels of engagement are encouraging (Disley et al, 2011).

The pilot project at HMP Peterborough is a world first. Predominantly foundations and charities with aims related to criminal justice have invested £5 million in the hope that reoffending will be reduced. If successful (defined as a reduction greater than 7.5 per cent measured against a control group; see Disley et al, 2011), such organisations will reap the financial benefits following from their initial investments, but also philanthropic benefits since it offers a 'mission-aligned' investment opportunity for many of the organisations that have offered financial support (Disley et al, 2011). In the case of the pilot, outcome payments will be made by the Ministry of Justice and the Big Lottery Fund, but given the wider savings made by the state when individuals do not reoffend (for example, reduced costs to the health service and policing), in future other government departments (for example, the Department of Health and Home Office) could be expected to contribute should positive outcomes be reported. The term 'bond' in this instance is rather misleading because the investment is not guaranteed, and failure to reduce reoffending will result in no recompense. This transfer of risk is particularly attractive to the government who under this model are not directly involved in commissioning or managing service providers.

A report entitled *Lessons learned from the planning and early implementation of the Social Impact Bond at HMP Peterborough* is available (Disley et al, 2011).

As the Coalition government itself acknowledges, PbR funding mechanisms can create perverse incentives (Ministry of Justice, 2010), with implications in terms of the equality of service provided to prisoners. This approach is designed to obtain the maximum outcome at the lowest cost (Whitfield, 2012), threatening resettlement work with the most 'needy' prisoners. There is the potential for 'parking' of the most disadvantaged, for example, problem drug users, prisoners with mental health problems or those with extensive criminal histories. Alongside this there is the risk of 'creaming' or 'cherry-picking' of the least challenging cases, for example, offenders who are able to return to their jobs and homes or those serving a prison sentence for the first time. In anticipation of this, the Green Paper states explicitly that measures will be introduced to ensure 'that providers are not allowed to choose which offenders their success will be measured against' (Ministry of Justice, 2010: 46). In addition, the Green Paper shies away from a 'one size fits all model' in two respects. First, it argues that PbR mechanisms may not be suitable for all groups of offenders, for example, the most serious and dangerous offenders subject to MAPPAs (see *Box 4.1*). Second, it recognises that independent providers might need to be encouraged to work with groups of offenders who may not be significant in terms of the overall numbers but who have specific needs. Examples given in this respect are female offenders and young adult offenders (that is, those aged 18–21). On 30 September 2012, they comprised 5 per cent and 8 per cent of the prison population respectively (Ministry of Justice, 2012a).

PbR projects must inevitably be accompanied by monitoring and evaluation, raising thorny issues about definitions of success in terms of outcomes and the most appropriate approaches for measuring those deemed successful. Potentially this could help to consolidate the evidence base relating to resettlement that remains patchy, making it difficult for investors to calculate with any certainty the likely return on their investment (for a more detailed discussion, see Fox and Albertson, 2011). However, a focus on outcomes without consideration of processes is problematic. We turn our attention to these issues in the next section.

Developing resettlement: an example of evidence-based policy?

There is now an abundance of projects operating across prisons in England and Wales, which is both a cause and effect of resettlement becoming of increased importance to policy-makers. These projects vary from small-scale projects working in one prison through to those operating across a region (for example, the SWing project which ran in prisons across the South West of England between 2003 and 2006; see Hudson, 2007) or nationally (for example, PS Plus, a large-scale prison-probation-based employment programme; see Cole et al, 2007). Many resettlement projects began life as 'pilot' projects. Accompanied by monitoring and evaluation, the intention was to explore the most effective ways of working in order to establish best practice, which could then be more widely disseminated once Custody Plus was introduced (see page 77). *Box 5.2* describes the Resettlement Pathfinders that comprised seven pilot projects. As noted in Chapter Three, pilots were a favoured approach by New Labour when introducing policies and modes of delivery that had yet to demonstrate they could be effective. If accompanied by rigorous evaluation they can provide evidence of effective practice to inform decisions about whether to 'roll out' interventions on a larger scale, and if so, what changes might need to be made to the initial design. A small-scale embryonic initiative requires a considerable investment of time and resources but reduces the risk – financial and otherwise – of introducing approaches that prove to be ineffective.

Box 5.2: The Resettlement Pathfinders

The Resettlement Pathfinders ran for six years, divided into two phases: the first comprised of seven projects and three of these continued into the second phase. The initial projects ran in seven prisons including one women's prison and one private prison (for men). They were designed to test out different approaches to working with prisoners, both in terms of the lead organisation, orientation and the underlying theory of how resettlement promotes desistance (Raynor, 2007). This resulted in three projects led by voluntary sector organisations that aimed to address prisoners' 'welfare' needs and create opportunities for them to lead law-abiding lives. Often this was done indirectly through 'signposting' prisoners to appropriate services (for example, housing providers). In contrast, the remaining probation-led projects focused on developing prisoners' thinking skills and pro-social attitudes in order to motivate participants to choose alternatives to offending. This was achieved through a groupwork programme, based on cognitive behavioural principles that were common to many 'what works' initiatives which originated in the early part of the 21st century (Raynor and Robinson, 2009). All projects in Phase One targeted adult prisoners serving short sentences, and this was largely true of Phase Two. Both phases were evaluated and the findings published (Lewis et al, 2003; Clancy et al, 2006). The evaluations focused not only on outputs and outcomes (for example, continuity of contract 'through the prison gate', changes in attitudes and self-reported problems and reoffending; improvements in accommodation, employment and problem substance use; and reconviction rates), but also on the implementation process. The 'Further reading' section at the end of this chapter includes references to the main publications that arose from the evaluation of the Resettlement Pathfinders. Additional publications include Lewis et al (2007) and Maguire and Raynor (2006).

The notion of 'effectiveness' with respect to criminal justice interventions is a contested one, although in policy terms it tends to be conflated with reducing reoffending. Even if it is accepted that reductions in reoffending are an appropriate measure of success, this opens up a debate about which data to use to measure reoffending and what might count as a successful outcome. In general terms, reconviction data (that is, convictions officially recorded) is used as a proxy measure for reoffending although evaluation has sometimes supplemented it with self-reported offending (see, for example, Clancy et al, 2006).

There has been an extensive debate about the appropriateness of this measure (see Lloyd et al, 1994; Mair et al, 1997; Friendship et al, 2002). Briefly the concerns are two-fold: first, the incomplete nature of the data is recognised since relatively few offences involve offenders being 'brought to justice' and official records do not include all minor offences committed, and second, the measure is seen as too crude. This is particularly relevant when referring to former prisoners, who may have entrenched criminal careers. It is widely acknowledged that desistance from offending is a process rather than a one-off event (see Farrall and Calverley, 2005). Comparing predicted and actual rates of reoffending for both the 'intervention' and 'comparison' groups (who have not benefited from participating in the project) is seen as good practice. This approach was used to evaluate the Resettlement Pathfinders described in *Box 5.2*. Even so, this measure still lacks sophistication. First, it does not identify differences in terms of the nature and/or extent of offending post-intervention. It can be argued that committing fewer offences is a successful outcome when working with a prolific offender or less serious offences for those with a history of involvement in violent crime. Second, while it is possible to make the 'intervention' and 'comparison' groups as similar as possible in terms of characteristics such as age, type of offence and so on, it is not possible to take into account all the different factors which may influence the desistance process. The latter challenge can be overcome by randomly allocating individuals to receive a particular intervention (or not), but this approach is very costly (since it requires a large number of participants), logistically difficult, and raises moral and ethical dilemmas (for a more detailed discussion, see Wincup and Hucklesby, 2007).

Given the criminal histories of many prisoners, focusing solely on reconviction rates as a measure of 'success' condemns many projects to 'failure', and alternative measures of success need to be sought. These tend to focus on changes in criminogenic needs, ranging from those that lend themselves more easily to measurable outcomes (for example, drug or alcohol use) through to those which are less tangible (for example, emotional wellbeing). The former are often prioritised and the Resettlement Pathfinders were unusual in that they also explored attitudinal change. The appropriateness of measures will vary from project to project, depending on its focus. For example, some resettlement projects have emphasised enhancing employability so it would be appropriate for outcomes to reflect the 'distance travelled' by participants in relation to employment, education and training. An important measure of success for resettlement work is what the Resettlement Pathfinders refer to as 'continuity of service', the proportion that continued to engage with the project beyond the day of release. In the new funding arrangements, this measure would be insufficient because it captures the process rather than its 'result'.

Despite over a decade of renewed emphasis on resettlement, the evidence base in relation to effective resettlement remains patchy, leading Wincup and Hucklesby (2007: 88) to call for more 'theoretically-informed, methodologically sophisticated and ethically sound' research designs. This claim is still valid as relatively little has been published on resettlement in the past five years. The introduction of PbR mechanisms into the delivery of resettlement services will encourage methodological sophistication with respect to measuring reoffending. However, unless this is accompanied by an understanding of the most appropriate processes for producing the desired outcomes, there is a danger that evaluating programmes becomes a technical exercise in which 'hard' quantitative evidence is favoured over 'soft' qualitative data. This creates little space to explore stakeholders' (for example, staff, volunteers, and most importantly, offenders) experiences of resettlement projects, assumes that interventions are implemented as planned (which was not the case with the Resettlement Pathfinders) and does little to develop the theory underpinning resettlement projects, which have too rarely drawn on desistance theory (Hedderman, 2007). Some of the most useful aspects of evaluations of 'pilot' or 'pathfinder' projects have been discussions of the difficulties of implementing resettlement projects, but too often, as Wincup and Hucklesby (2007) note, organisations have not been willing to do so. Once contestability was introduced, evidence about what works and what does not became commercially sensitive (even for voluntary sector organisations). Organisations began to search for the 'Holy Grail' of definitive statements that their particular model of resettlement work was effective in reducing reoffending, and in so doing glossed over how an individual's post-release experience was heavily influenced by factors outside their control. These include policy agendas relating to welfare provision, even though supporting former prisoners to negotiate their way through bureaucratic practices associated with them is a core part of the everyday work of resettlement project staff and volunteers. We turn our attention to these in the final section of this chapter.

Social policy and prisoners

The final section of this chapter explores two important aspects of work to resettle prisoners: namely, finding suitable accommodation and enhancing the employability of former prisoners. In the *Reducing reoffending: National action plan* (Home Office, 2004b) these are the first and second pathways, reflecting the important contribution that appropriate housing and employment make to the process of desisting from crime.

Securing accommodation

The role of appropriate housing in preventing further reoffending is widely recognised, although as Maguire and Nolan (2007: 145) argue, it is important to appreciate that addressing former prisoners' accommodation problems is a '*necessary*, if not a *sufficient*, condition for the reduction of reoffending' (original emphasis). The notion of appropriate housing is contested, but typically makes reference to the stability of an individual's accommodation. Prisoners often experience precarious living arrangements before custody and on their release: the 2003 Resettlement Survey revealed that 14 per cent of prisoners were living in temporary accommodation or sleeping rough prior to being imprisoned, and 29 per cent of those interviewed expected to be released (in three weeks or less) to these living arrangements (Niven and Stewart, 2005). Given the widely documented housing problems experienced by prisoners (for an overview, see Maguire and Nolan, 2007), and the lower reconviction rates among offenders with stable accommodation (May, 1999; Howard, 2006), it is unsurprising that addressing housing problems has become a key focus for resettlement projects. For some prisoners, the situation appears to be relatively straightforward in that they are able to return to their own homes. However, we should not assume that this inevitably provides stability or that it is appropriate. For example, it might involve returning to live with a partner after a lengthy time in custody where the future of the relationship is uncertain, or returning to an area where criminal networks are likely to threaten the process of establishing a law-abiding lifestyle. A more likely outcome is that they will need to search for new accommodation unless specific arrangements are made by criminal justice agencies for them to live at a specific address; for example, offenders from whom the public is in need of protection might be asked to reside in approved premises, essentially a hostel run by either a probation trust or a voluntary sector organisation which offenders are directed to live in.

To obtain social housing, individuals need to ensure that they fulfil certain criteria. Local authorities are not required to provide housing for all those accepted as homeless (for a discussion of housing legislation aimed at non-lawyers, see Lund, 2011), and those most likely to be provided with housing (which initially is often temporary housing) are those who can demonstrate 'priority need'. The main groups in this respect are those with dependent children, pregnant women, those who are vulnerable (for example, due to their age or physical and mental health) and victims of emergencies such as floods or fire. Consequently, relatively few prisoners are likely to be defined as priorities for housing since the majority of those who leave prison each year are male, relatively young and single, as noted elsewhere in this chapter. Since the introduction of the Homelessness Act 2002, some prisoners have been included in the priority need category, but it only applies to those deemed vulnerable as a result of imprisonment. Vulnerability is a subjective concept. The onus is on the applicant to prove their vulnerability when applying to English authorities, but secondary legislation (see page 10 for an explanation of this term) in Wales has resulted in prisoners automatically being perceived as vulnerable by virtue of their status (for more details, see Maguire and Nolan, 2007). Monitoring the impact of the 2002 amendment on prisoners' access to housing is difficult because official statistics do not provide sufficient detail. However, the limited evidence available suggests little has changed in practice in England (Allender et al, 2005). Young adult prisoners may benefit more from the inclusion of care leavers aged 18 to 20 in the list of priority groups given that prisoners are over 13 times more likely to have to spend time 'in care' than the general population (Social Exclusion Unit, 2002).

Applicants also need to demonstrate that they have a local connection with the area in which they wish to be allocated housing. Prisoners can be disadvantaged in numerous ways by this requirement. First, it encourages individuals to return to criminogenic communities rather than make a 'fresh start' elsewhere. Second, it does not allow the prisoners to try and establish lives near the prison in which they have been accommodated, from which they may have already set up links with local organisations. Finally, prisoners are less likely than the public more generally to be able to demonstrate a local connection in terms of employment and/or family relationships. The 2003 Resettlement Survey (Niven and Stewart, 2005) found that just under one third of prisoners had education, employment and training arranged for release. Moreover, they found that 15 per cent of prisoners had no contact with their family and 3 per cent had no family at all.

In order to be accepted for housing, applicants also have to *not* fulfil certain criteria. These promote the notion that the 'right' to housing – under tightly defined circumstances, as explored above – is conditional on whether individuals respect their responsibilities as citizens. This theme runs through many contemporary social policies, and we return to it in the concluding chapter. First, they have to prove that they have not made themselves intentionally homeless. This means that applicants need to ensure that they deliberately did (or didn't do) something that caused them to leave accommodation that they could have otherwise remained in, and in which it would have been reasonable for them to do so. A recurring theme within welfare provision is the distinction between the 'deserving' and the 'undeserving', and this criterion is used to distinguish between those who had no choice to leave their accommodation (for example, they were subject to domestic violence) and those who were evicted due to their own actions (for example, non-payment of rent or engaging in anti-social behaviour). Potentially those imprisoned for offending who then go on to lose their accommodation might be seen as making themselves intentionally homeless. Second, but related to the above, applicants need to ensure they do not fulfil the behaviour condition set out in the Homelessness Act 2002. It allows a local authority to treat an applicant as ineligible for housing if they are satisfied that the individual (or a member of their household) has been found guilty of unacceptable behaviour serious enough to make them unsuitable as a tenant. A safeguard is in place that means local authorities must be satisfied that the behaviour remains a current concern. Prisoners, perhaps more than any other group, are most likely to fall foul of this condition.

This succinct overview of social housing policy illustrates how prisoners might be both advantaged and disadvantaged by the current allocation rules, although as Maguire and Nolan (2007) argue, more often than not it is the latter. Given the difficulties of securing access through local authorities, the majority of those leaving prison become reliant on the voluntary sector since relatively few can meet the requirements demanded by private landlords in terms of upfront rental payment, financial bonds and reference checks, and they may be excluded for other reasons, for example, because they are claiming Housing Benefit. Voluntary sector organisations play a pivotal role in terms of promoting access to accommodation and/ or providing it directly through both emergency accommodation such as night shelters and hostels for those who are 'roofless' and supported accommodation for people making the transition to independent living. Once more, criteria need to be fulfilled since accommodation may only

ered to those who have particular demographic characteristics
ample, only available for women or young people) and who are
d to comply with the particular conditions attached to living in the
nodation provided (for example, willing to engage in education or
training). Particular groups of former prisoners (for example, current drug
users or problem drinkers) may find themselves excluded from multiple
projects.

Enhancing employability

Like appropriate housing, taking steps to enhance the employability of
offenders is seen as essential to supporting an offender to desist from
crime. The argument made by Maguire and Nolan (2007: 145, original
emphasis) that accommodation is 'a *necessary*, if not a *sufficient*, condition
for the reduction of reoffending' applies equally to employment. Typically
many prisoners were unemployed prior to entering prison, and fewer still
are able to obtain employment on release. The 2003 Resettlement Survey
found that over two thirds were not engaged in education, employment
and training prior to entering custody, and a similar proportion did not
have anything arranged for their release (Niven and Stewart, 2005). Given
high levels of unemployment among prisoners and the close connection
between employment and lower reconviction rates (May, 1999; Howard,
2006), understandably enhancing employability has become an important
focus of resettlement work, with some resettlement projects – as already
noted – making this their primary focus. Such efforts sit comfortably
with the political emphasis on promoting work as the primary duty of
responsible citizens.

Welfare reform has been a political priority for successive governments.
The Coalition government inherited from its predecessor a welfare-to-
work agenda that attempted to encourage, enable and increasingly require
individuals to enter employment. A series of 'New Deals' were introduced,
focusing initially on young people aged 18 to 24 and later on groups of
benefit claimants who had not been expected to seek paid work in the past,
such as lone parents and those with disabilities. Collectively they aimed
to promote 'active welfare', requiring individuals to take responsibility for
seeking employment rather than being 'passive' recipients of welfare. This
'welfare contract' releases relatively few from these conditions, for example,
those with poor physical and mental health and those with responsibility
for caring for young children. For the vast majority the receipt of state
benefits is conditional on taking steps to secure employment: failing to
do so results in benefit sanctions. In many respects there is evidence of
political consensus in relation to welfare-to-work measures, which is widely

recognised (see Deacon and Patrick, 2011). However, the Coalition has presented its measures in terms of radical reform. The Conservative–Liberal Democrat government was quick to introduce a Welfare Reform Bill that received Royal Assent in 2012 after a protracted passage through Parliament. Universal Credit has been in place since April 2012, an integrated welfare payment system for those of working age, which is attempting to improve work incentives, simplify the benefits system and tackle administrative complexity (see DWP, 2010), alongside even more controversial measures such as introducing caps on the total amount of benefit that can be paid. These reforms, alongside the introduction of the Work Programme (described below), attempt to ensure that as many individuals as possible enter the labour market, or at least engage in work-related activity, which is believed to have transformative properties (see Deacon and Patrick, 2011), including reducing the risk of reoffending.

The Work Programme is a five-year welfare-to-work initiative introduced by the Coalition government, and has been described as a 'step change' (see DWP, 2011) compared to New Labour's programme of promoting active welfare. The Work Programme is also an example of PbR that uses a contract based on incentive payments, mirroring practices deployed in the NHS. A small initial fee is awarded to the service provider for each new starter, and further payments are dependent on their success in supporting individuals to both obtain and retain employment (for an introductory overview, see Whitfield, 2012). These payments are funded through the savings associated with someone ceasing to claim out-of-work benefits and contributing financially through the payment of tax and National Insurance to the government. It is envisaged that the focus on outcomes, coupled with encouraging competitiveness between potential providers, will promote value for money. Under this model, the Department for Work and Pensions is responsible for commissioning service providers and setting minimum delivery standards, but service providers are largely free to deliver what they consider to be the most appropriate interventions to help individuals overcome the barriers to entering the labour market and remaining within it. There are tensions here between the government rhetoric of a personalised approach for those trapped in the cycle of welfare dependency, and the rather crude funding mechanisms which take no account of the appropriateness of the employment for individuals in terms of their skills and needs.

For individuals who are mandated to participate in such programmes (which last up to two years) as a condition of claiming Universal Credit, the 'carrot' of employment support – which may not be realised in practice – is accompanied by a 'stick', the loss of benefits if requirements attached to participating in the programme are not fulfilled. Requirements are set by the 18 prime providers – mostly from the private sector – that are delivering the Work Programme in 40 regions in England. These prime providers subcontract other organisations to provide specialist employment support, for example, to those with disabilities. ***Box 5.3*** describes the specialist provision put in place for prisoners.

Box 5.3: The Work Programme for prisoners

In March 2012, the Department for Work and Pensions announced the launch of a dedicated Work Programme for prisoners, to operate in England, Wales and Scotland (DWP, 2012), and pilots began in June 2012. Targeted at those claiming Jobseeker's Allowance while in custody (or up to 13 weeks post-release), it requires prisoners to participate in the Work Programme from the day of their release (or immediately after they make their claim) rather than fulfil the referral criteria (that is, being unemployed for over six months in the case of 18- to 24-year-olds and over 12 months for those aged 25 and over). Service providers are expected to provide support while in custody. Success in terms of this Work Programme is a former prisoner obtaining employment and retaining it for two years, resulting in an incentive payment for the service provider of £5,600 (DWP, 2012). This is considerably less than the £6,600 maximum payment available to those who are the most seriously disadvantaged in the labour market (DWP, 2011). The pilots will explore how reoffending might be included as an outcome measure (Ministry of Justice, 2011b).

Supporting prisoners to obtain employment is a laudable aim, and securing employment is an aspiration for the majority. Indeed, as one study found, prisoners often had 'high hopes' in this respect which were difficult to realise on release (Hartfree et al, 2008). The 2003 Resettlement Survey found that of the 70 per cent of prisoners who did not have education, training or employment arranged for their release, three quarters hoped to do so (Niven and Stewart, 2005). However, there has been little discussion to date about how prisoners might be supported to overcome the barriers they are likely to face as applicants with relatively few skills or qualifications and disrupted or no work histories, alongside their criminal convictions (see Metcalf et al, 2001; Rolfe, 2001; Fletcher, 2003). The Rehabilitation of Offenders Act 1974 offers some assistance to offenders: with certain exceptions (for example, if applying for posts working with children or related to national security), the majority of those who offend are in a position where they do not have to declare their prior involvement in crime after a set period of time. Convictions that resulted in a prison sentence of over two and a half years (moving to four years from Spring 2013) are never spent, so the

Act provides relatively little protection from discrimination for significant proportions of those released from custody each year. There has also been insufficient discussion as to how attempts to enhance the employability of former prisoners might 'join up' with other interventions individuals may be participating in (for example, supervision by probation in the case of offenders who are sentenced to more than 12 months in custody) and how service providers will manage the wide range of difficulties faced by former prisoners which have a significant impact on attempts to promote access to education, employment and training, such as problem substance use and housing difficulties.

Summary

- Resettlement has grown in importance as a policy issue since 1997, but there remains a lack of provision, particularly for short-term prisoners.
- The voluntary sector has always been heavily involved in resettling prisoners alongside criminal justice agencies, but is likely to play a greater role in the future.
- Private sector involvement in resettling prisoners is likely to grow significantly.
- There remain significant gaps in our understanding of 'what works' in relation to resettling prisoners.
- While social policies in the areas of housing and employment can both include and exclude prisoners, they are predominantly exclusionary.

Questions for discussion

- What factors help to explain New Labour's interest in enhancing resettlement policies for prisoners?
- What are the advantages and disadvantages of promoting (a) voluntary sector and (b) private sector involvement in resettlement services?
- What have been the most influential factors in the development of resettlement policy and practice?
- How might social policies have an impact on prisoner resettlement?

Further reading

- Clancy, A., Hudson, K., Maguire, M., Peake, R., Raynor, P., Vanstone, M. and Kynch, J. (2006) *Getting out and staying out: Results of the Resettlement Pathfinders*, Bristol: The Policy Press – presents the findings of the evaluation of the second phase of the Resettlement Pathfinder.
- Hucklesby, A. and Hagley-Dickinson, L. (2007) *Prisoner resettlement: Policy and practice*, Cullompton: Willan Publishing – this edited collection provides 'a

comprehensive review and analysis of resettlement policy and practice in England and Wales in the early part of the 21st century' (see back cover).

- Lewis, S., Vennard, J., Maguire, M., Raynor, P., Vanstone, M., Raybould, S. and Rix, A. (2003) *The resettlement of short-term prisoners: An evaluation of seven Pathfinders*, RDS Occasional Paper No 83, London: Home Office – this report presents the findings of the evaluation of the first phase of the Resettlement Pathfinder and is available online at http://webarchive.nationalarchives.gov.uk/20110220105210/rds.homeoffice.gov.uk/rds/pdfs2/occ83pathfinders.pdf

- *Criminology and Criminal Justice* (Volume 6, Number 1) is dedicated to exploring life after imprisonment and focuses on problems, prospects and possibilities.

Readers are also advised to look at the policy documents referenced throughout this chapter.

Guide to electronic resources

- **Depaul UK** (www.depauluk.org) is a national charity that works with young people who are homeless, vulnerable and disadvantaged. Founded in 1989, it is a good example of an organisation that became involved in the resettlement of prisoners through its knowledge and expertise in a related policy area (in this instance, homelessness).

- **Nacro** (www.nacro.org.uk) is a crime reduction charity which works with people before, during and after they are in trouble across England and Wales (there are similar organisations for Scotland [Sacro] and Northern Ireland [NIACRO]). The resettlement of prisoners is an important dimension of its work. A chapter by Hucklesby and Worrall in Hucklesby and Hagley-Dickinson (2007), detailed above, explores Nacro's involvement in three resettlement projects, including the Resettlement Pathfinder described in *Box 5.2*.

- **Prison Reform Trust** (www.prisonreformtrust.org.uk) is a penal pressure group (see Chapter Three) which aims to reduce the use of imprisonment, develop more effective prison regimes for those whose offending is so serious they have to be incarcerated and to educate the public, politicians and sentencers about criminal justice. The resettlement of prisoners is one of its project areas.

- **St Giles Trust** (www.stgilestrust.org.uk) is also a national charity and, like Depaul UK, its roots lie in working with homeless people. Today it aims to break the cycle of offending, crime and disadvantage. This charity was involved in the pilot resettlement project described in *Box 5.1*.

six

The messy realities of policy-making: tackling the drug 'problem'

Overview

This chapter focuses on the messy realities of drug policy-making. Using drug policy as a case study it brings alive the issues explored in Chapter Three by elucidating the multiplicity of influences on policy statements that are encapsulated periodically in strategic documents. We explore the tensions, and sometimes conflict, which stem from two issues. First, while there is a consensus, to some extent, that drugs are a 'problem', there is a lack of agreement on the nature of the 'problem', and as a result competing, if not contradictory, policy solutions are proffered. Second, drugs continue to be an area of intense political interest (Measham and South, 2012), and at times the stated commitment to evidence-based drug policy appears compromised as governments pursue highly symbolic drug policies underpinned more by political ideology than science. Since drugs is also an area of personal interest (Measham and South, 2012), this has resulted in a lack of support for current policies among some members of the public.

Key concepts

Abstinence, coercion, (de)criminalisation, experimental drug use, evidence, harm reduction, legalisation, partnership working, problem drug use, recovery, recreational drug use

Drug use: constructing a 'problem'

This chapter is concerned primarily with 'problem' drug use. In policy terms, this refers to the use of heroin and/or crack cocaine. Within government discourse around these drugs it is assumed that using them is a problem, particularly for wider society. There is no attempt to recognise that heroin can be used occasionally and not involve dependency, or be used regularly in a manner which is controlled (Warburton et al, 2005), or that similarly, many users of crack cocaine do so only on an irregular basis (DrugScope, 2010). While practitioners and academics recognise the links between particular drugs and problematic use, in defining problem drug use their focus is on patterns of usage rather than the actual drugs used. For these professionals, drug use becomes a 'problem' when it involves dependency, regular excessive use (leading to risk of overdose) or use which exposes users to serious health risks (for instance, through injecting) or other risks, which might be social, psychological, physical or legal (see Advisory Council on the Misuse of Drugs, 1998). Examples of 'other' risks include children been taken into care, drug-induced psychosis, assault when purchasing drugs and being arrested. Not least because of the lack of an agreed-on definition of problem drug use, it is difficult to identify the precise number of drug users who might fall into this category. As a proxy measure we might include those currently accessing drug treatment. This includes those who have defined their own use of drugs as problematic and, as we explore later in this chapter, those whose drug use has been categorised in this way by state agencies, principally criminal justice ones.

On October 2012 there were almost 200,000 drug users in England accessing drug treatment (National Treatment Agency for Substance Misuse, 2012a). This figure does not capture all problem drug users and it is estimated that there are just over 300,000 problem drug users in England (National Treatment Agency for Substance Misuse, 2012a). The latter figure is calculated using data obtained from a range of agencies that problem drug users (defined here as users of heroin, methadone, other opiate drugs or crack cocaine) come into contact with including the police, prisons, probation and drug treatment agencies (Hay et al, 2011). This group is predominantly male (77 per cent) and aged 25 and over (85 per cent). In terms of risky behaviours, just over one third are estimated to be injecting drug users (and thus a potential threat to public health), and at least one quarter are poly drug users.

Problem drug use is typically distinguished from 'experimental' and 'recreational' drug use. In many respects these terms are based more on individual opinion than on accepted definitions (Wincup and Traynor, 2013), but we can offer some working definitions. Recreational drug use is typically centred on the use of cannabis, 'party' drugs (now most commonly cocaine powder, but in the recent past, ecstasy) and increasingly legal highs. These new substances are widely available on the internet, as well as through other outlets such as 'head shops', and are designed to mimic the effects of illegal drugs. At least from the perspective of those who use drugs recreationally, their use of drugs is not risky. Even though it might be regular and frequent (for example, every weekend), it does not involve dependency in a physical sense, although it might be argued that since drug use forms part and parcel of an individual's use of leisure time, abstaining might be difficult. Experimental drug use refers to drug taking which is short-lived and does not form an integral part of an individual's life. It can vary from a one-off event, for example, someone trying cannabis at a party where a joint is being passed around, through to experimentation with a greater variety of drugs.

Data from the Crime Survey for England and Wales 2011/12 (Home Office, 2012b), arguably the best source of data on self-reported drug use (for a more detailed discussion of its relative strengths and weaknesses, see Wincup and Traynor, 2013), paint a picture of widespread experimentation, and in some instances, ongoing use. It found that approximately 37 per cent of adults (aged 16–59) had ever taken an illicit (and in most instances illegal) drug in their lifetime, falling to 9 per cent in the previous year, and 5 per cent in the last month. In raw numbers, this refers to population estimates of approximately 12 million, nearly 3 million and 1.7 million, respectively. These figures illustrate that those defined as problem drug users represent only a small proportion of current drug users. By far the most commonly used drug was cannabis, followed by cocaine powder (not crack).

Box 6.1 identifies some of the characteristics of 'typical' drug users as identified by the Crime Survey for England and Wales using data related to use in the previous year. Even a cursory glance at these characteristics reveals that a wide range of social groups are engaged in drug use. Unlike problem drug use, which has strong links with social exclusion (Foster, 2000; Neale, 2006), recreational drug users or experimenters are sometimes individuals who are closely integrated into society. Information on the characteristics of drug users/triers can be useful when developing drug prevention programmes since it provides some insight into the groups that could be targeted. Such approaches, as we explore in the next chapter in a different policy setting, can be problematic for two reasons: there is a real possibility of excluding those who might be at risk, and an unintended consequence of such interventions might be to stigmatise particular groups.

Box 6.1: Characteristics associated with drug use

- Male
- Aged 16–24
- White or mixed race
- Single or cohabiting
- Students or unemployed
- Frequent visits to pubs/clubs
- Frequent drinkers

It is difficult to 'pigeonhole' people into one particular category of drug use, and individuals may move from one to another throughout their drug-using careers. For example, experimental drug use might lead to more sustained recreational drug use, or more rarely, problem drug use. Similarly, a former problem drug user may abstain from what are often referred to as 'hard' drugs (for instance, heroin) while continuing to use 'soft' drugs (for instance, cannabis) on a recreational basis. For example, Wincup et al's (2003) study of young homeless people revealed that rather than abstaining from all forms of drug use, some former problem drug users used different drugs on a recreational basis. It is also important to underline that in many senses *all* drug use is problematic because of the health risks involved – although their precise nature is often disputed – and because of the potential for contact with criminal justice agencies.

So far we have used the term 'problem' rather loosely and largely in terms of the impact on an individual drug user rather than society. Before moving on to explore strategic approaches to tackling the drug 'problem', we should stop and explore the different ways in which drugs are problematic. The drug 'problem' has been defined as a law and order, medical, public health and social problem (see Wincup, 2011), as summarised in *Table 6.1*. These different interpretations have, at different times, influenced the development of UK drug policy since policies are shaped by the way a 'problem' is perceived (MacGregor, 2010). Indeed, at any one time drug policy may not reflect the divergent interests of the range of professional groups who view the drug 'problem' through different lenses but who are tasked with 'solving' it together. For example, research on the street policing of problem drug users (see also *Box 2.4*) found that policing strategies – which were heavily reliant on displacement and exclusion – clashed with the efforts of agencies to establish ongoing supportive relationships with local problem drug users (Lister et al, 2008).

Table 6.1: Divergent interpretations of the drug 'problem'

Nature of the problem	Identified concerns	Proposed solutions
Law and order	Connections between drug use and crime are emphasised, both in terms of offending by problem drug users, and also crime associated with the drugs trade	• Reducing the supply of drugs through enforcement activity at all levels • Reducing the demand for drugs among offenders through treatment
Medical	Drug use can be conceptualised as a 'disease', which has severe consequences for the health of an individual	• Drug treatment
Public health	Drug use can have negative effects on the health and wellbeing of communities, for example, through discarded drug paraphernalia and spread of disease such as Hepatitis	• Needle exchange schemes • Drug consumption rooms (not in the UK)
Social	Connections between drug use and social exclusion (New Labour) or social problem (Coalition) are emphasised	• Drug prevention • Reintegration of problem drug users • Responsibilisation of problem drug users

Strategic approaches to the drug 'problem': emerging trends

While the drug 'problem' has a long history (see Barton, 2003), it was only in the mid-1980s that the first genuine strategic response was developed in England (Home Office, 1985). This was followed 10 years later by a White Paper. *Tackling drugs together* (Home Office, 1995) laid the foundations for successive drug strategies by moving drug policy further away from harm reduction (see Monaghan, 2012). Defining problem drug use as a 'medical' and 'public health' problem (see *Table 6.1*), drug policy focused on containing rather than eradicating the problems caused predominantly by injecting drug use(rs) through measures such as needle exchange schemes and substitute prescribing. Most significantly, *Tackling drugs together* created Drug Action Teams (described in *Box 6.2*) to facilitate partnership working across the range of organisations whose expertise might be drawn on to tackle the drug 'problem', now largely defined in terms of 'law and order'.

This brought criminal justice agencies into the fold to address drug use in the hope that this would lead to reductions in crime rates.

Since then four further drug strategies have been published over a 12-year period, three by the New Labour governments and the latest by the Coalition government (President of the Council, 1998; Home Office, 2002; HM Government, 2008, 2010b). Below we offer a potted history of these strategic developments and also consider the key official players in both the development and implementation of drug policy (see ***Box 6.2***). Before going further it is important to emphasise that the discussion is focused predominantly on England, although the situation is not so clear-cut as this for two main reasons, First, some of the strategies have claimed to include Britain (President of the Council, 1998) or the UK (Home Office, 2002), even though in practice their main focus is on England. Second, and specifically relating to Wales, tackling drugs cuts across a number of policy areas such as crime control which the Welsh Government does not have overall responsibility for (see page 5). Consequently, its strategic responses to the drug 'problem' are influenced by developments at Whitehall.

> ## Box 6.2: Drug policy-making and implementation: identifying the key official players
>
> - The **Advisory Council on the Misuse of Drugs** was established following the implementation of the Misuse of Drugs Act 1971, and is tasked with keeping under review the drug 'problem' and providing advice to ministers. At present it comprises 22 members from a range of professional areas including pharmacy, policing, medicine, law, higher education and the drugs field. In 2009, five members resigned following the dismissal of its chair, Professor David Nutt, for critical statements about the reclassification of cannabis (see ***Box 6.5***) (Nutt, 2009). His controversial sacking opened up considerable debate about the willingness of ministers to listen to advice provided by experts, and raised questions about their autonomy (see Chapter Three for a discussion of the role of experts in policy-making).
> - **Drug Action Teams** were created in 1995, and there are currently 149 in England with responsibilities for coordinating and commissioning services and performance management. They are a further example of a multi-agency partnership described in ***Box 4.1***.
> - The **Home Office** is currently the lead department on drug policy. There have been repeated calls for other government departments to take a lead role. In 2007, the RSA (Royal Society for the encouragement of Arts, Manufactures and Commerce) recommended that responsibility for drug policy be moved to the Department for Communities and Local Government. More recently, the Home Affairs Committee (2012) recommended that the Home Secretary

and the Secretary of State for Health should have joint overall responsibility for drugs policy.

- The **Inter-ministerial Group on Drugs** includes representatives from eight government departments (Home Office, Education, Health, Ministry of Justice, Work and Pensions, Communities and Local Government, Cabinet Office and HM Treasury). It aims to drive forward and oversee implementation of the drugs strategy through the promotion of an inter-departmental approach. The Home Affairs Committee (2012) requested greater transparency in relation to the workings of this group.

- The **National Treatment Agency for Substance Misuse (NTA)** was established in 2001 as a special health authority to improve the availability, capacity and effectiveness of drug treatment in England. Its remit included the allocation of resources, provision of support and guidance and monitoring. In April 2013 it was incorporated into Public Health England, a clear example of the Coalition government following through on its intention to reduce significantly the number of quangos (see page 34). In keeping with pursuit of the localism agenda (see page 68), decisions about which drug services to fund will become the responsibility of Police and Crime Commissioners.

Shortly after New Labour came to power in 1997, a far-reaching strategy was published. *Tackling drugs to build a better Britain* (President of the Council, 1998) attempted to lay out the broad trajectory of drug policy for the next decade. It had four elements relating to young people, communities, treatment and availability. This is in keeping with the tripartite approach of drug policy, operating in the spheres of prevention, treatment and enforcement, even though it has been suggested that this can result in 'duplication of work, missed opportunities for increased effectiveness through working together and feelings of institutional protectionism' (UK Drug Policy Commission, 2012: 11). The strategy also explicitly stated the six principles on which it was based, which were highly reflective of New Labour's approach to tackling social problems. These included a focus on social exclusion, a commitment to evidence-based policy and an emphasis on partnership working. Responsibility for implementing the strategy was moved from the Home Office to the Cabinet Office to facilitate joint working across government departments. In many respects this was a symbolic move since the strategy was developed by Keith Hellawell, dubbed the drugs Tsar, whose background as a former chief constable heavily influenced its direction. This strategy provided a clear indication of what was to follow by emphasising the apparently causal links between problem drug use and high levels of involvement in crime, despite a wealth of criminological research that has accentuated the need for a nuanced understanding of this relationship (see, for example, Bennett and Holloway, 2007).

Four years later, in 2002, the Home Office – and note the change of authorship – published an updated strategy, six years before its predecessor's 'best before' date. It was not an attempt to start 'from scratch' (Home Office, 2002: 3); rather it aimed to sharpen the focus and to improve strategic effectiveness. Most significantly, it prioritised working with problem drug users – in practice, users of heroin and crack cocaine – who were perceived to pose the greatest risk of harm to themselves and their communities. Exploiting the opportunities provided by the criminal justice process to tackling problem drug use among known offenders was a core component of the strategy. The continued criminalisation of drug policy has had a major impact on how criminal justice agencies, in partnership with drug treatment providers, process drug-using offenders, and we shortly consider how this strategic alignment of drug policy and crime policy has been operationalised over the past decade. In essence, it has led to a large number of offenders – some of whom had not sought help before – being channelled, and sometimes coerced, into drug treatment programmes. We pick up the story of how drug policy has evolved over the past five years later in this chapter. Before doing so we look more closely at the criminalisation of drug policy, and in particular, the mechanisms used to increase the number of drug-using offenders accessing treatment.

Drug policy and crime control: carrots and sticks

As already noted, during the 1980s and most of the 1990s, medical models of drug use (viewed in terms of disease and addiction) dominated drug policy. These were joined later by an emphasis on the promotion of public health as a response to the HIV/AIDS crisis and recognition of the harm caused by unsafe injecting practices. While drug services did work with those who offended, they did not work closely with criminal justice agencies, and relied on offenders to self-refer. Specific provisions included in the Criminal Justice Act 1991 to make drug treatment a condition of a Probation Order were rarely used, mostly due to fundamental opposition on ethical and ideological grounds to the principle of coerced treatment which was seen to be at odds with the ingredients of effective rehabilitation (Duke, 2010). High levels of motivation were perceived to be essential to successful treatment, which those coerced into treatment could not be expected to have. Subsequent research, as we explore shortly, has challenged this assumption.

As the new millennium drew closer, the drug 'problem' was increasingly connected with the crime 'problem', and accordingly, what Stevens (2011:

77) refers to as the 'socio-political construction of drug-related crime' became the fundamental driver of drug policy. This was incorporated into strategic thinking, becoming most influential in 2002. This approach assumed that drug users and offenders are most commonly one and the same, and that there is a direct and causal link between drug use and crime. It was also the catalyst for the expansion and investment in drug treatment opportunities within the criminal justice system (MacGregor, 2010). Initially beginning with voluntary interventions such as arrest referral schemes (see Mair and Millings, 2010), this quickly gathered pace, extending into a full range of essentially coercive drug treatment activities, now coordinated through the Drug Interventions Programme (see *Box 6.3*).

Box 6.3: The Drug Interventions Programme

The Drug Interventions Programme (DIP) was launched in 2003, initially in England and later in Wales. It aims to provide an integrated approach for adult users of Class A drugs throughout the criminal justice process, from the pre-trial stage through to the resettlement of offenders, in the hope that promoting access to drug treatment will reduce drug-related offending. Consequently, it involves police forces, the criminal courts, probation trusts and prisons working in partnership at a local level with providers of drug treatment and social support (for example, housing). It is estimated that DIP costs £150 million a year to administer, and works with between 4,000 and 4,500 problem drug users (excluding prisoners) each year (figures for 2009–10) (National Audit Office, 2010). DIP includes the following interventions (for a critical review of research evidence on the range of interventions that form the Programme, see Hucklesby and Wincup, 2010):

- *Drug testing on charge and on arrest:* drug testing for individuals charged with 'trigger' offences (that is, those which are most commonly drug-related) was introduced by the Criminal Justice Act 2003, and similar provisions were introduced for those arrested by the Drugs Act 2005. Those testing positive for heroin and/or crack cocaine must attend a mandatory 'required assessment'. Further support is available via arrest referral schemes.
- *Restrictions on bail:* this places an obligation on courts to implement a bail condition compelling defendants who test positive for heroin and/or crack cocaine to engage in treatment for the duration of their court bail.
- *Conditional cautions:* since 2003, offenders can be required to participate in drug treatment as a condition of a police caution.
- *Drug Rehabilitation Requirements:* these were introduced in the Criminal Justice Act 2003 and replaced Drug Treatment and Testing Orders which began in 1998. Like their predecessor they require offenders to participate in a drug treatment programme as part of their Community Order, but can

be combined with other requirements (see Worrall and Canton, 2013). They can also form part of a Suspended Sentence Order.

- *CARAT* (Counselling, Assessment, Referral, Advice, Throughcare) schemes have operated in all prisons across England and Wales since 1999. They aim to provide drug treatment while in custody, which continues 'through the prison gate' (see Chapter Five).

Bold claims have been made about the success of the programme by Home Office researchers (Skodbo et al, 2007), although independent research suggests the evidence is less unequivocal (Turnbull and Skinns, 2010). Nonetheless official endorsement might account for DIP's longevity and the large-scale investment, although in a climate of scarce resources, and given the lack of public support for financing drug treatment, funding for drug treatment is increasingly under threat (Measham and South, 2012). From April 2013 DIP will no longer receive central funding, and local programmes will have to convince their Police and Crime Commissioner (see page 64) to devote resources to drug interventions.

The widespread use of drug interventions with individuals caught up in the criminal justice process is based on an assumption – seemingly supported by evidence – that treatment 'works' (see National Treatment Agency for Substance Misuse, 2012b). Alongside considerable investment in drug treatment, the government has invested considerable resources in evaluating drug treatment, most notably through the National Treatment Outcome Research Study (NTORS) and Drug Treatment Outcome Research Study (DTORS). The most widely quoted finding based on this is that £1 spent on drug treatment results in a saving of between £2.50 and £3 given the high costs associated with problem drug use, particularly associated with drug-related offending. Presented as an indisputable 'fact', successive governments have been able to use it as a lever to secure funding from HM Treasury for resource-intensive programmes such as DIP. Evidence from DTORS also offers tentative support for quasi-compulsory drug treatment. The available evidence does not allow bold claims to be made that legal or formal coercion does or does not work, but does undermine the argument that treatment inevitably does not work if individuals are directed to access it via the criminal justice process (Jones et al, 2009). At the same time, findings from NTORS challenge the very premise on which DIP is founded, namely, that there is a causal link between problem drug use and offending (Gossop, 2005), echoing the findings from other studies which have examined the relationship between drugs and crime (see, for example, Bennett and Holloway's 2007 research with arrestees).

There is now an extensive literature on both the principle of coercion (see Seddon, 2007) and the effectiveness of coercive approaches (see Stevens,

2010). Essentially programmes such as DIP require 'offenders' (including those who have yet to be found guilty of any offence) to make 'tough choices'. Even those aspects of the programme which are technically voluntary in that an individual has to agree to drug treatment are quasi-compulsory in the sense that failing to comply can lead to less favourable outcomes, for example, being given a custodial sentence rather than a community penalty. Therefore unlike compulsory drug treatment activities that are used in other countries (Harm Reduction International, 2010), individuals have to provide consent, but for many, it is a 'Hobson's Choice' since the alternatives are far from attractive. While there are 'carrots', principally immediate access to drug treatment (a particular incentive in the past when waiting lists for drug treatment were lengthy), there are also 'sticks', which can ultimately mean the loss of liberty.

The use of coercion no longer attracts the same degree of criticism that it did in the late 1990s (see below) and has become widely tolerated, if not accepted, practice, in working with drug-using offenders. In many respects, coercive drug treatment appears to offer a 'third way' to the challenges of balancing treatment and punishment. It provides a 'meeting point' for proponents of the medical and law and order models, although supporters of the former have taken time to grow accustomed to the notion of coercion within decisions about healthcare interventions which are ordinarily based on freely given consent. These concerns resurfaced following the proposal to link drug treatment to the payment of welfare benefits in the 2008 drug strategy (see Wincup, 2011b). Once again, a stark contrast was made between 'voluntary' and 'coerced' treatment. It is assumed that self-referring clients make choices free from external influences while those directed to treatment by state agencies lack motivation. In practice the boundaries are blurred, for example, those self-referring may have been directed to undergo treatment by family members.

Towards recovery: a new agenda for drug policy?

In 2008, the New Labour government published a further drug strategy, *Drugs: Protecting families and communities* (HM Government, 2008). Much was familiar about this strategy. Once again it emphasised the need to break the links between drugs and crime by taking advantage of the full range of treatment opportunities that can be offered to individuals as they progress through the criminal justice process. However, two potentially distinct aspects are worth noting. First, it emphasised once more the need to promote the social inclusion of drug users, which was present in the 1998 strategy but glossed over when it was updated in 2002. Second, it gave greater prominence to the families of drug users, reflective of a broader agenda that is the focus of our next chapter. When the 2008 drug strategy was still in its infancy, the new Coalition government swiftly published their own strategic thinking on drugs entitled *Drug strategy 2010: Reducing demand, restricting supply, building recovery: Supporting people to live a drug free life* (HM Government, 2010b).

Recent analyses of strategic thinking on the drug 'problem' have posed questions about a possible change of direction that commenced under New Labour and gathered momentum with the creation of the Coalition government (Monaghan, 2012; Duke, 2013). A recurring theme within these analyses is the disjuncture between political discourse, with its emphasis on a 'fundamentally different approach' (HM Government, 2010b: 3) and practice, which has seen little attempt to dismantle the emphasis placed on crime reduction that has characterised drug policy for the past two decades. As Duke (2013: 12) argues, 'the criminal justice system remains in a pivotal position'. However, we should reflect on three apparent shifts within policy. The first relates to the questioning of the mechanisms by which criminal justice agencies, in conjunction with drug treatment providers, have sought to manage drug-using offenders. The heavy reliance on substitute medication, particularly methadone, has been brought into question on the grounds that it replaces one dependency with another (see Monaghan and Wincup, forthcoming). A commitment to abstinence as the goal of recovery is therefore the distinguishing feature of much political discourse, as influenced by think tanks (see **Box 6.4**). The 2010 drug strategy reflected a more diluted and pragmatic position, attempting to appeal to proponents of harm reduction and abstinence-based treatment (see Duke, 2013), and also to square the circle of the desirability of abstinence approaches and the lack of resources available for expensive forms of abstinence-based residential treatment (see Monaghan, 2012). The second concerns the increased emphasis on the links between worklessness and drug use. This is reflected in proposals to make the payment of out-of-work welfare benefits to problem drug users conditional on engaging in work-related activity, which might include drug treatment. However, the sociopolitical construction of drug-related worklessness has yet to displace the priority attached to tackling drug-related crime. Instead, it heightens stigmatisation of problem drug users by categorising them as irresponsible and dependent non-citizens. This provides further evidence of what Monaghan (2012: 29) terms a 'creeping moralisation' within social policy. The final issue relates to the mechanisms by which drug treatment is funded, and here we begin to see clearer evidence of a departure from the past. Taking further proposals contained in the Green Paper *Breaking the cycle: Effective punishment, rehabilitation and sentencing of offenders* (Ministry of Justice, 2010), in April 2011 drug (and alcohol) recovery pilots were developed in eight local areas across England, funded on a PbR basis (as discussed in the previous chapter). These are expected not only to deliver in terms of positive drug outcomes – defined in terms of abstinence – but also in relation to offending, employment, and health and wellbeing.

Box 6.4: Promoting abstinence: the role of think tanks

Over the past six years, think tanks (as defined on page 36) have been prominent in drug policy-making. In particular, they have influenced heavily the shift from harm reduction towards abstinence, at least in an ideological sense, even if this is not always realised in practice. Two think tanks in particular have played a pivotal role, whose work we describe below.

- The Centre for Social Justice (described on page 37) published a report entitled *Addictions towards recovery* (note the terminology used, which deploys a medical model of drug use) as part of its *Breakthrough Britain* series (Centre for Social Justice, 2006b). This report makes the audacious claim that the government drug strategy has failed, not least since it continues to promote harm reduction through the use of community-based drug treatment reliant on the use of substitute medication. Consequently, it claims reforming drug policy is a Herculean task. On its website it lists 10 policy proposals, some of which have already been incorporated into drug policy, at least in part. They include the reclassification of cannabis (see **Box 6.5**), piloting of dedicated drug courts and the establishment of drug recovery wings in prison. They also argue for the expansion of residential rehabilitation. While this was advocated in the *Programme for government* (HM Government, 2010a), the level of financial investment required to support this has not been forthcoming, and almost all problem drug users (prisoners aside) are treated via community-based services. At an ideological level, we can see clearer evidence of this think tank's commitment to notions of 'abstinence' and 'recovery' in government discourse about drug treatment.
- The Centre for Policy Studies was established in 1974 by Margaret Thatcher (prior to becoming Prime Minister five years later) and Keith Joseph (a Conservative MP and Cabinet member under Thatcher). It therefore has strong historical links with the Conservative Party, but describes itself as independent and non-partisan. Its overarching philosophy is the promotion of free market economics. In 2008, it set up a Prison and Addiction Forum that published a report that was highly critical of the harm reduction approach to drug treatment. The title of the report – *Breaking the habit: Why the state should stop dealing drugs and start doing rehab* (Gyngell, 2011) – epitomises its thinking. Authored by Kathy Gyngell, who also wrote the Centre for Social Justice's (2006) report on addiction (described above), it promotes

abstinence-based rehabilitation. She argues that the Coalition's approach to recovery is well intentioned but doomed to failure since it does too little to free individuals from addiction.

Legislation: part of the problem or part of the solution?

We can trace attempts to control drug use back to the Pharmacy Act 1868 which, for the first time, regulated drug markets by restricting the sale of opium to pharmacists. Thus, in some respects, subjecting drugs to legal control is a relatively recent development, driven by both moral and practical logic (Shiner, 2006). Throughout the 20th century a series of laws were introduced to strengthen drug legislation relating to the import, export, possession, use, manufacture and distribution of drugs, but the most significant reform was in 1971 when the Misuse of Drugs Act was introduced. This Act replaced somewhat vague references to 'dangerous' drugs with the language of control by attempting to permit appropriate use of drugs in medical contexts while prohibiting their illicit use. The level of control, and consequently the penalty for misuse, was expected to be proportionate to the degree of harm each drug was believed to pose. To operationalise this, drugs were divided into three categories: Class A (the most harmful) through to Class C (the least harmful). Over 40 years on, the Act continues to provide the statutory framework for the control of drugs despite considerable criticism, explored later in this section. It has, however, been updated (for example, to respond to new drugs emerging and shifts in official perceptions of harmfulness; see *Box 6.5*) and supplemented by additional drug laws such as the Drugs Act 2005 and more general crime control legislation.

At the same time as outlining the state's response to illicit drug use, the Act serves as a 'social control tool with which to promote and ensure conformity with a drug-free lifestyle' (Barton: 2003: 51). The principle of harmfulness provides the philosophical basis of the drugs law (Ruggerio, 1999), but the inclusion of particular substances rather than others in drug legislation reflects official perceptions of relative harmfulness at a specific moment in history (Measham and South, 2012), and public perceptions of harmfulness may not accord with those enshrined in legislation. This is vividly illustrated by the reclassification of cannabis, twice over a five-year period, explored in *Box 6.5*. Making objective judgements about harmfulness is challenging, both in terms of collecting reliable scientific evidence but also because of the high level of political interest that surrounds illegal drugs. Consequently, as Measham and South (2012) argue, in addition to considering pharmacology (the science that deals with the origin, nature, chemistry, effects and uses of drugs), it is crucial to explore the social, economic, political and personal context to drug use.

Box 6.5: Shifting sands: (re)classifying cannabis

In 2004, cannabis was downgraded from a Class B to a Class C drug. Four years later, the Home Secretary at the time, Jacqui Smith, made the decision to return cannabis to its former class, and in 2009 it became, once more, a Class B drug. The situation is aptly characterised by Stevens (2011: 129) through the metaphor of a 'yo-yo'. The initial decision to reclassify cannabis was in many respects evidence-based. It was influenced by an independent inquiry into the Misuse of Drugs Act 1971, conducted by the Police Foundation (a further example of a think tank; see Chapter Three) which was supported by further inquiries conducted in 2002 by the Home Affairs Committee and the Advisory Council on the Misuse of Drugs (see *Box 6.2*). The final report (Police Foundation, 2000) advocated for a less punitive approach to possession offences and a more punitive approach to those involving supply. The majority of possession offences are for cannabis, which, following its move to Class C, no longer remained an arrestable offence in the majority of circumstances. Instead, cannabis warnings were introduced as a further example of summary justice (see page 14). This move was supported by research findings (May et al, 2002) that suggested that reclassifying cannabis might have positive instrumental and expressive effects. First, it could potentially free up police time to respond to other demands, which might include policing Class A drugs. In this way, it was consistent with New Labour's commitment to modernise criminal justice (described in Chapter Four) and the updated drug strategy (Home Office, 2002). Second, it might remove a source of friction between the police and particular communities. Subsequent research revealed that these aspirations were not fully realised in practice (see May et al, 2007). The decision to return cannabis to its former class was a controversial one. It was justified on the grounds that newer forms of cannabis (skunk) were more harmful, posing real threats to mental health. This contradicted the findings of a public consultation that supported cannabis remaining a Class C drug (Ipsos MORI, 2008) and went against the advice of the ACMD (2008) and in so doing triggered a dispute between the New Labour government and its scientific advisers.

The decision to reclassify cannabis for the first time was also influenced by practice 'on the ground', illustrating that even 'top-down' policy-making can be responsive to 'bottom-up' calls for change. This was typified by the Lambeth pilot scheme, launched by the Metropolitan Police in 2001. This was essentially a policy of implicit decriminalisation by using on-the-spot warnings rather than criminal sanctions for possession offences (for a more detailed discussion of the scheme and its impact, see Crowther-Dowey, 2007).

Debates about whether the current legislative framework is fit for purpose have repeatedly taken place over the past 12 years, although its intensity has waxed and waned. Helpfully summarised by Stevens (2011: 132–4) in a detailed table, there have been five influential reports by think tanks, charities and campaigning groups which have argued for either significant reform of the Misuse of Drugs Act 1971 or its replacement. The former (what Shiner, 2006: 63, refers to as 'the revisionist critique') retains the commitment to the principle of harmfulness enshrined in drug legislation, while the latter (which Shiner, 2006: 65, describes as 'the radical assault') highlights the counter-productive nature of drug policy, which exacerbates the risks associated with drug use.

At the end of 2012, the debate intensified following the publication of two significant reports. The first was the final report of the UK Drug Policy Commission (described on page 111) entitled *A fresh approach to drugs*, which argued that the process of classifying controlled drugs should be reviewed with a view to: creating an expert body with a statutory role to make classification decisions; reducing sanctions for drug possession; reviewing penalties for all drug offences; and developing an integrated framework to control the supply of all psychoactive substances, including alcohol, tobacco, solvents and performance-enhancing drugs. The second was a report by the Home Affairs Committee, which, among other issues, looked at the Misuse of Drugs Act 1971. Using once again the metaphor 'breaking the cycle', it recommended that a Royal Commission (see page 32) be established to conduct 'a fundamental review of all UK drugs policy in the international context' which would report by 2015 (Home Affairs Committee, 2012). As policy-makers so frequently do (see Chapter Three), the Committee looked beyond the UK to consider whether any policy might be transferred from elsewhere.

It examined in the greatest detail the shift towards decriminalisation that has taken place in Portugal. In 2001, the Portuguese government decriminalised the use and possession of all illicit drugs. Following a recommendation by a government-appointed Expert Commission, criminal sanctions were replaced with measures to identify dependent drug users and to steer them towards treatment. Research (see Hughes and Stevens, 2010) suggests that this bold step did not lead to the substantial increases in illicit drug use that opponents feared. The Home Affairs Committee report was sufficiently sensitive to cultural differences to avoid proposing direct policy transfer, but it advocated that the UK government visit Portugal to examine its system of depenalisation and emphasis on treatment. Predominantly because of this, the report received a mixed response from politicians (causing disagreement between the Prime Minister and his Deputy) and the media coverage focused on this at the expense of other issues in the report, which ranged from education and prevention through to drugs in prison. This refuelled the debate about whether the criminalisation of particular substances creates harm rather than protects individuals and communities from it. This debate has included conservative, liberal and radical commentators who oppose drug prohibition laws for distinct reasons that coalesce around a disdain for state interference in the ability of individuals to make personal choices (Ruggerio, 1999). For Stevens (2011), the polarised debate between legalisation and prohibition – which has been explored in depth elsewhere (see, for example, Bean, 2008; McKeganey, 2011) – has reached stalemate. He suggests that rarely have the social constraints, alongside legal ones, which influence individual 'choices' about drug use, been considered. Arguably, the social context in which drug use takes place is far more pervasive than the legal framework.

The Home Affairs Committee (2012) report also explored the implications of the rapidly growing market in 'legal highs'. Since their emergence as a problem in 2009 when mephedrone (now a Class B drug) came to the attention of both the police and the public, these have presented a challenge for drug legislation. Widely available at low cost and without the legal risk associated with the drugs they were designed to mimic, these synthetic psychoactive substances quickly became a popular drug of choice among different groups of young people: those aged under 18 experimenting with both legal and illegal drugs and more drugwise recreational drug users (for an overview of the emerging literature, see Measham and South, 2012). A moral panic ensued when mephedrone was associated with the deaths of young people in 2009/10. This resulted in the criminalisation of mephedrone in 2010 and proposals – now implemented – in the Coalition's *Programme for government* (HM Government, 2010a) to introduce 12-month temporary bans on such substances while the Advisory Council on the Misuse of Drugs (see *Box 6.2*) decided whether they should be permanently controlled. This was incorporated into the Police Reform and Social Responsibility Act 2011 under the banner Temporary Class Drug Orders, and used for the first time in March 2012. These Orders were heavily criticised by the Home Affairs Committee (2012), which argued that the market was moving too rapidly for the current system to keep up since on average at least one new substance is discovered each week. As an alternative the Committee proposed greater use of existing trading standards and consumer protection legislation to help local authorities take action against businesses that currently sell these untested products without consequence, by labelling their products as unfit for human consumption.

Summary

- There remains considerable debate about the nature and extent of the drug 'problem' and the most appropriate 'solutions'.
- Successive drug strategies have defined drug use as a law and order 'problem', although in practice it has always been a far more wide-ranging 'problem' requiring a partnership of criminal justice, health, welfare and drug treatment agencies to work together to offer 'solutions'.
- Coercion is now widely accepted, or at least tolerated, as a policy response to tackling problem drug use.
- Drug use is a highly politicised issue: the collision of evidence and politics contributes to the contentious nature of drug policy-making.
- Close examination of drug policy is needed to reveal the ways in which different interests are reconciled (or not), and to identify points of disjuncture between political rhetoric, policy and practice.

Questions for discussion

- Why has tackling problem drug use become a priority for criminal justice agencies? What are the implications of this?
- Does criminalisation protect potential drug users from harm, or increase their vulnerability?
- What are the barriers to developing evidence-based drug policy?
- Who are the key players in the development and implementation of drug policy?

Further reading

- Monaghan, M. (2011) *Evidence versus politics: Exploiting research in UK drug policy making?*, Bristol: The Policy Press. Drawing on interviews with key players in the policy-making process, this monograph uses the example of cannabis to draw out the role of evidence in the creation of drug policy.
- Stevens, A. (2011) *Drugs, crime and public health: The political economy of drug policy*, London: Routledge. This offers a critical discussion of recent policy on illicit drugs, centred on the UK, but deploying a comparative approach.
- Hucklesby, A. and Wincup, E. (eds) (2010) *Drug interventions in criminal justice*, Buckingham: Open University Press. This edited collection explores the range of drug interventions that operate at all stages of the criminal process to channel drug users into treatment.
- MacGregor, S. (ed) (2010) *Responding to drug misuse: Research and policy priorities in health and social care*, London: Routledge. This book brings together essays on drug treatment, including a chapter on the focus of crime and coercion in UK drugs policy.

Guide to electronic resources

- **DrugScope** (www.drugscope.org.uk) is the UK's leading independent centre of expertise on drugs and the national membership organisation for the drug field. Its website offers a 'mine of information' on drugs and drug policy.
- **Students for Sensible Drug Policy** (http://ssdp.org) is a grassroots student-led organisation based in the US but with a global presence. It does not condone or advocate drug use but emphasises the importance of encouraging young people to engage in the political process, and advocates the importance of individual choice.
- **UK Drug Policy Commission** (www.ukdpc.org.uk) aims to bring evidence and analysis together to inform drug policy. Its website provides access to its research reports plus its submissions to government to influence the policy process.
- The **UK Harm Reduction Alliance** (www.ukhra.org) is a campaigning coalition of drug users, health and social care workers, criminal justice workers and educationalists that aims to put public health and human rights at the centre of drug treatment and service provision for drug users. Its website provides access to its attempts to have an impact on policy-making through statements, responses to consultations and so on.
- Many organisations in the drugs field use **Twitter** to publicise their work. Use the search facility available within Twitter to locate suitable organisations to follow.

seven

'Troubled' or 'troublesome' families? Social policy and crime prevention

Overview

In November 2011, the Coalition government launched the Troubled Families programme, promising to turn around the lives of 120,000 families by the end of their first term of government (likely to be 2015). 'Troubles' in this context refers, somewhat controversially (as we explore towards the end of the chapter), to involvement in crime and anti-social behaviour, truancy and school exclusion, dependence on out-of-work benefits and 'high costs to the public purse' (CLG, 2012b: 3). This programme represents yet another attempt by successive governments to prevent crime through working with families. This gathered pace under New Labour, but prior to 1997, research had highlighted the role of the family in protecting young people from crime or exposing them to heightened risk. This filtered through to influential official reports that advocated policy change (see, for example, Audit Commission, 1996). Since 1997, a range of approaches has been used. They have included services available to all such as Sure Start which is not simply focused on crime reduction but has a far broader remit, for example, to reduce child poverty and to promote health and wellbeing through to more coercive approaches designed to 'responsibilise' parents whose children are already engaged in criminal and/or anti-social behaviour (including truancy; see Chapter Two). In between are targeted interventions at those perceived as most likely to offend. Through exploring examples of each, we consider the relative strengths and weaknesses of universal and targeted approaches to prevent youth offending through family interventions.

Like the previous two chapters, this one uses the example of family interventions to explore wider issues which should now be familiar to readers of this book, for example, evidence-based policy, partnership working and the use of PbR mechanisms to fund services. We also explore, once more, the role of coercion in regulating the behaviour of those judged to be 'troublesome' (see also Chapter Six).

Key concepts
Anti-social behaviour, developmental crime prevention, early intervention, evidence-based policy, family, PbR (Payment by Results), partnership working, protective factors, responsibilisation, risk factors, social exclusion, targeting

Conceptualising the 'family'

At its most basic, the 'family' is typically thought to comprise of a small, intimate group of people who are living together in which the adults are responsible for the care and socialisation of children. This describes the 'nuclear' family, which forms the core of most known societies (Bruce and Yearley, 2006). It can be distinguished from the 'extended' family that refers to a larger group (who are unlikely to be living in the same household) that includes more than two generations and/or kin with whom there is a less proximate relationship (for example, aunts, uncles, cousins). It is often asserted that the 'extended' family is in decline, but this has been questioned through historical and contemporary research (Bruce and Yearley, 2006). Closer examination questions the dominance of the extended family during periods characterised by low life expectancy. It also highlights how better transport links and the growth of technology (for example, telephone, email, social media) have allowed family members to keep in close contact. Similarly, higher rates of life expectancy, at least for the most affluent members of society and especially women, have afforded grandparents the possibility of spending more time with their grandchildren, sometimes playing an active role in providing childcare. There is, however, a shared view that 'the family' has become more complex, from the mid-20th century onwards. During this period, lone parenthood (sometimes following the breakdown of a relationship) and cohabitation have become more common. Consequently, a significant proportion of children are now growing up in households headed up by one individual or an unmarried couple (see *Box 7.1*). Further evidence of diversity relates to the growth of gay families, and reconstituted or blended families, principally through parents forming new relationships, for example, following divorce.

Box 7.1: Families in contemporary Britain

- Two fifths of people are married and live with children
- Less than 10 per cent of the population are cohabiting and live with children
- The average number of children in a family (of all types) is 1.7
- Almost one quarter of families with dependent children are headed by a lone parent, usually a mother (only 3 per cent of families with dependent children are headed by a lone father)
- Lone parenthood has increased significantly over the past four decades, but the proportion has been relatively stable since the mid-1990s
- Over half of lone mothers are widowed, divorced or separated

Source: ONS (2011)

The family has been studied through a range of theoretical lenses (for a brief overview, see Cheal, 2011), many of which have been developed through critical engagement with the functionalist perspective, particularly as advanced by the American sociologist Talcott Parsons. From this perspective, the nuclear family is best suited to regulating sexual relations, reproduction, the socialisation of children and economic cooperation between the sexes (Bruce and Yearley, 2006). This has been challenged by sociologists from different theoretical traditions who have questioned these assumptions and drawn attention, for example, to issues such as power relations and inequality, and its manifestation in forms of violence, predominantly against women and children (Saraga, 2001).

Many of the policies explored in this chapter have been developed in response to the view that some families are dysfunctional or problematic. Some policy advocates have been keen to describe particular family forms in this way. For example, the Centre for Social Justice, a think tank (see page 37), has expressed concern about family breakdown, a concept which it uses to refer to dysfunction, dissolution (separation and divorce) and 'dad–lessness'. Consequently, it aims to promote marriage through incentives in the tax and benefits system (see Centre for Social Justice, 2012). The justification is that marriage brings stability. This proposal has the support of the current Prime Minister, David Cameron, and there is some evidence that this position has begun to have an impact on government policy. However, it is not a universally held view across the Coalition government. We began this book by discussing the riots that took place in a number of cities across England in the summer of 2011. In his speech to the Conservative Party conference, Iain Duncan Smith argued that the main causes of the urban disturbances were family breakdown alongside welfare dependency (Mulholland, 2011), which echoes the work of Charles

Murray (1990), a US political commentator who has written extensively about the 'underclass' characterised by illegitimacy, welfare dependency and violent crime. More recently, references to dysfunction made their way into another speech by Iain Duncan Smith, who proposed that family stability should be incorporated into indicators of child poverty (Wintour, 2012).

We should not, of course, dismiss the evidence that certain family forms appear to be related (albeit not in a direct or causal sense) to an increased likelihood of criminal and/or anti-social behaviour, alongside other social problems such as child poverty and poor educational outcomes. Since the 1960s and particularly since the mid-1990s, criminologists have sought to identify the range of risk factors associated with crime and anti-social behaviour, which has had a significant impact on policy and practice. We explore this work in the next section.

Risk factors for crime and anti-social behaviour

Since 1961, when the Cambridge Study for Delinquent Development began, criminologists from across the UK have been concerned with identifying risk factors associated with offending, mostly through longitudinal studies, as illustrated in *Box 7.2*. Similar studies have been conducted in North America, Scandinavia and New Zealand, producing remarkably similar findings (see Farrington, 2007). The focus was initially on males since they commit a disproportionate amount of crime and in particular, the most serious offences (see Heidensohn and Silvestri, 2012). However, more recent studies have included females in their samples, contributing to a debate about whether risk factors are gender-specific (for a review of relevant research, see Moffit et al, 2001; McAra, 2005). While women are of less interest because of their small contribution to offending, they are of great interest because of their relative conformity – exploring the factors which influence why women conform might inform prevention techniques, although we should not assume that 'what works' for women can be translated to men.

> **Box 7.2:** Exploring pathways into and out of crime through longitudinal research: key UK studies
>
> The Cambridge Study of Delinquent Development is a survey of 411 males that began in 1961–62 when the boys were aged between 8 and 9. At the time, all the participants were resident in a working-class area in London and were attending secondary school (with 12 attending what was referred to at the time as schools for those who were educationally 'subnormal'). Since then there have been regular follow-ups, which at different points have involved collecting data

from participants, their parents and teachers, alongside criminal record checks (see www.crim.cam.ac.uk/people/academic_research/david_farrington/hofind281. pdf). The study has been influential in advocating the growth of risk-based prevention activities, including parenting programmes.

The **Edinburgh Study for Youth Transitions and Crime** (www.law.ed.ac.uk/ cls/esytc/) began in 1998, and follows a cohort of around 4,000 young people from Edinburgh who started secondary school (and were therefore aged 11) that year. Unlike earlier studies, the sample includes males and females in an attempt to understand gender differences in patterns of offending. Some of the earliest publications from the study explored the link between crime and parenting, using data gathered from the young people about their experiences of being 'parented'.

Risk factors can be defined as individual attributes or characteristics, situational conditions or environmental contexts that increase the probability of problematic behaviour occurring, or increasing in intensity or severity (adapted from Clayton, 1992). Risk factors are typically divided into two categories: 'static' and 'dynamic'. The former refers to attributes that cannot be changed, for example, gender; more controversially, some might also include genetic influences and biological mediators on this list (for an introductory overview of the links between biology and criminal behaviour, see Hopkins Burke, 2009). The latter – a much longer list – are those which can be modified in order to prevent the development of criminal careers. It is important to note that none of the factors operate in isolation; indeed, many are closely related, and a challenge for criminologists is to consider the 'cumulative, interactive and sequential effects of risk factors' (Farrington, 2007: 604).

Risk factors are typically categorised across four domains: family, school, community and individual/personal. *Table 7.1* lists the risk factors that the Youth Justice Board (2005) understand to be associated with offending, while noting that similar factors are also predictive of problem substance use, educational underachievement, young parenthood and adolescent mental health problems.

Research on risk factors has had a significant impact on policy and practice. It has underpinned the growth of 'developmental crime prevention' (Tremblay and Craig, 1995), offering the potential for early intervention to prevent offending, or at least to confine it to a small number of minor offences. Such interventions target not only risk factors but also protective factors, defined similarly as individual attributes or characteristics, situational conditions or environmental contexts that inhibit, reduce or buffer problematic behaviours.

Table 7.1: *Risk factors for youth offending*

Family	• Poor parental supervision and discipline • Conflict • History of criminal activity • Parental attitudes that condone anti-social behaviour and criminal behaviour • Low income • Poor housing
School	• Low achievement beginning in primary school • Aggressive behaviour (including bullying) • Lack of commitment (including truancy) • School disorganisation
Community	• Living in a disadvantaged neighbourhood • Disorganisation and neglect • Availability of drugs • High population turnover, and lack of neighbourhood attachment
Personal	• Hyperactivity and impulsivity • Low intelligence and cognitive impairment • Alienation and lack of social commitment • Attitudes that condone offending and drug misuse • Early involvement in crime and drug misuse • Friendships with peers involved in crime and drug misuse

The extensive international research on risk factors for offending has drawn attention to the importance of 'the family'. These can be loosely divided into four categories. The first relates to parenting, which, as we explore later in the chapter, has been the focus of many interventions. This includes poor supervision; harsh or punitive discipline, coldness and rejection; and low parental involvement with children (see Farrington, 2007). At the extreme, this might involve child abuse in all its forms (physical, sexual and emotional). The second set of factors is socioeconomic, and refers to low income and poor housing. As we explore in the next section, successive governments have attempted to tackle child poverty but have yet to make significant inroads (see Joseph Rowntree Foundation, 2012). The third category comprises factors associated with family forms. In his review of the literature on family risk factors, Farrington (2007) draws attention to the recurrent findings that large family size is a relative strong predictor of offending, and similarly, disrupted families (often referred to as 'broken homes'). His analysis of explanations for these findings emphasises the need to avoid simplistic explanations. For example, it may be that economic deprivation, exacerbated in large families, is the key factor, or that the presence of conflict between parents has a greater impact than the 'broken home'. As we have already witnessed, this nuanced understanding has not always been reflected in political discourse, which has appeared to stigmatise particular family forms, for example, lone parents. Finally, the literature emphasises the intergenerational transmission of criminal and/or anti-social behaviour, and similarly, the negative influence of older siblings. There are numerous explanations for the finding that 'crime runs in families' (Farrington, 2007: 614). Theories that may not be mutually exclusive highlight the role of genetics (although not in a biological deterministic sense), drawing attention to the transmission of socioeconomic disadvantage between generations and poor parenting.

The focus on parenting as a risk factor for crime is not, of course, new. As Goldson and Jamieson (2002) describe, it can be traced back to the early 19th century, when what they described as the 'parenting deficit' was viewed as a cause of juvenile delinquency. What is distinctive, they argue, is the punitive edge of contemporary youth justice policy in its attempts to 'fix' it, which we explore later in the chapter when we consider interventions with the parents of children engaged in crime and/or anti-social behaviour.

Preventing (re)offending

Within the crime prevention literature, there is a heavy reliance on the tripartite conceptual framework developed by Brantingham and Faust (1976). Drawing on models adopted in both medicine and public health, they distinguished between primary, secondary and tertiary prevention activities.

- **Primary prevention** activities are directed towards general populations rather than specific groups. They aim to address risk factors in order to prevent a problem such as criminal or anti-social behaviour occurring.
- **Secondary prevention** activities involve working with 'at risk' groups. The presence of risk factors and/or absence of protective factors justifies this more targeted approach.
- **Tertiary prevention** activities focus on those who have already behaved in criminal or anti-social ways with a view to reducing the length of their criminal 'career' and preventing involvement in even more harmful acts.

These three categories of intervention are discussed in turn below. The framework is useful in that it distinguishes between different forms of crime prevention and allows us to incorporate policies that are most commonly categorised as social rather than crime policies. However, as we explore, policies do not always fit neatly into each of the three categories, and within a category there might be very different policies that do not at first glance appear to be connected. Criminologists have therefore sought to develop the conceptual framework, also distinguishing, for example, between policies that are oriented towards victims or offenders, and sometimes also communities (see Crawford, 1998). The policies discussed below are in some respects examples of offender-oriented crime prevention activities. However, it is important to recognise that boundaries between offenders and victims are sometimes blurred. For example, as already noted, victimisation can be a risk factor for offending.

Primary prevention

A wide range of initiatives has sought to make an impact on factors known to be linked with crime and anti-social behaviour in order to prevent them ever occurring. This might involve interventions even before a child is born. While not explicitly focused on the reduction of crime and anti-social behaviour, these initiatives have the potential to make a significant impact on crime rates as well as aspiring to other positive outcomes, including reductions in health and educational inequalities. Examples include:

- Tackling child poverty (for example, Child Tax Credits, Sure Start grants to expectant mothers on a low income)
- Promoting the employability of parents (for example, New Deal for Lone Parents and Working Tax Credits)
- Increased access to childcare (for example, funded nursery places for pre-school-aged children).

These measures are far from uncontroversial (see Churchill, 2012) and can be linked to broader political agendas to 'encourage' individuals, and some might argue, especially women, to acknowledge their responsibilities to engage in paid work and to make the transition from welfare to work. Paid work under New Labour became valorised, with politicians emphasising its potential to transform not only the lives of employees, but their children too (see Patrick, 2011).

It would, however, be misleading to underplay the commitment of New Labour to improving the life chances of children and young people. The influential Green Paper (DfES, 2003), *Every Child Matters*, which was the precursor to the Children Act 2004, aimed to develop a network of services from which all children could benefit but which would support in children most at risk (in a broad sense), such as looked-after children, children growing up in poverty and children suffering from abuse. This thinking underpinned the Sure Start programme and is described in *Box 7.3*.

Box 7.3: Sure Start

Sure Start was a flagship New Labour government programme that aimed to prevent social exclusion and to improve the life chances of pre-school children. It formed part of a more extensive strategy to work with children and families, which, as well as enhancing service provision, included greater financial support, helping families to balance work and home (Glass, 1999). Its origins lie in the 1998 Comprehensive Spending Review that established a series of departmental reviews and six cross-cutting reviews (including criminal justice). Sure Start arose out of the review of services for young children (for a detailed 'insider' account of the process by the leader of the inter-departmental review, see Glass, 1999). The review involved exploring international evidence of 'what works', principally from North America.

The programme was established with £452 million of funding to create 250 programmes throughout England in relatively small areas (comprising between 400 and 800 pre-school children). Two years later additional funding was provided to double the number of local programmes. The programme was expected to be non-stigmatising, multifaceted, persistent, locally driven, culturally appropriate and sensitive, and to involve parents *and* children (Glass, 1999). Local programmes aspired to provide services in a coordinated way through a network of public and voluntary sector agencies working in the fields of health, early education and family/parenting support.

The principles underpinning Sure Start (for a succinct but obviously not impartial discussion by the Director of the Sure Start Unit, see Eisenstadt, 2002) have much in common with New Labour's broader political approach: a commitment to user involvement illustrated through parental involvement, an emphasis on partnership working from government level down to area level (including coordination between other area-based initiatives), central coordination through the setting of explicit objectives and targets and a commitment to evidence-based policy. Under the leadership of Gordon Brown there was some move away from this approach. Most significantly, in 2003, he announced that responsibility for Sure Start would transfer to local authorities that became responsible for ensuring that a children's centre was located in every community. At this stage the national evaluation was incomplete since the programme had initially been established for a 10-year period.

Sure Start has grappled with the very tension discussed earlier in the chapter, namely, whether services should be targeted at those most in need of them or whether opening up services to all would allow those who needed them most to do so without feeling stigmatised. Its aspiration was to combine targeted

...es with open access by developing services in the most deprived areas ...lowing all, and in practice mainly mothers, residing within 'pram-pushing ...ce' (Clarke, 2006: 705) to use them. This tension came to the fore following ...nange of government in May 2010. The Coalition government introduced ...cant changes to Sure Start, which have attracted much criticism, not least because the most recent evaluation demonstrated beneficial effects in terms of family functioning and maternal wellbeing, although not specifically for children (NESS, 2012).

There are two main areas of controversy. The first relates to universal access. David Cameron has argued that this runs the risk of services being monopolised by the 'sharp-elbowed middle classes' (Hope, 2010). In their *Programme for government* (HM Government, 2010a: 19), the Coalition government announced that it would 'take Sure Start back to its original purpose of early intervention, increase its focus on the neediest families, and better involve organisations with a track record of supporting families'. The second area of controversy relates to funding which local authorities are no longer required to ring fence, and which may be funded through a PbR model (see Chapter Five). The first pilots were launched in July 2011.

The example of Sure Start illustrates how primary prevention activities can be viewed as benefiting those who are judged not to need help and therefore might be regarded as an inefficient use of scarce resources. It does, however, highlight some of the difficulties associated with identifying 'at risk' groups explored in the next section. Initiatives such as Sure Start can be portrayed in a positive light as programmes that strengthen protective factors and help families to build up resilience rather than crime prevention activities that seek to fix 'deficits'.

Secondary approaches

Since they target those most 'at risk' of offending, secondary prevention activities are attractive to policy-makers in search of cost-effective solutions. However, despite their appeal, targeted approaches are, in many respects, highly problematic. Not least, they challenge the principle of universalism that is embedded in many aspects of welfare provision, although this is increasingly under threat. A pertinent example, given our concern with families in this chapter, is that from January 2013 Child Benefit has been means tested for the first time in its 66-year history.

In 2006, the Social Exclusion Task Force was created, replacing the Social Exclusion Unit established by New Labour shortly after coming into power. It shifted the emphasis on to identifying and then working with a small minority of the most excluded groups, such as children with parents in prison (Social Exclusion Task Force, 2006). The Task Force's first report presented the findings of its Families at Risk review (2007). While recognising that parents could act as a source of resilience, it identified 14 parent-based risk factors including crime, anti-social behaviour, drugs and domestic violence. The review estimated that there were 140,000 families in England who were likely to experience inter-generational cycles of poor outcomes since their lives were characterised by at least five out of seven risk factors:

- no parent in the family in work;
- family living in poor quality or overcrowded housing;
- no parent has any qualifications;
- mother with mental health problems;
- at least one parent has a long-standing limiting illness, disability or infirmity;
- family with low income (below 60 per cent of the median); and
- family cannot afford a number of food and clothing items. (DCSF, 2009: 16)

It was suggested that this small minority of families – 2 per cent of families within England – would need intensive support. In practice, this has been targeted less at those who meet the criteria specified above and more at those who are engaged in criminal and/or anti-social behaviour, thus redefining tackling social exclusion in terms of preventing offending (Churchill and Clarke, 2010). We return to this issue in the final section of this chapter when we explore the current focus on 'troubled' families. For Churchill and Clarke (2010) there has been a conflation of two areas of policy interest: children 'at risk' of becoming socially excluded and children who constitute 'a risk' to society (Churchill and Clarke, 2010: 43). This provides further evidence of the criminalisation of social policy (see Chapters One and Two).

Identifying those most at risk of offending is, in many respects, highly problematic. First of all, there are practical challenges. It is difficult to identify those who might benefit most from intervention, and using proxy indicators to do so runs the risk of treating groups of people with the same characteristic as homogeneous. As two members of the Edinburgh Study for Youth Transition and Crime team have argued, 'early identification of at-risk children is not a water-tight process' (McAra and McVie, 2010: 189). Perhaps inevitably some of those 'at risk' will not be identified as in need of intervention, particularly since the target group is a fluid one. Families, for example, may move in and out of poverty and/or employment or between different forms of temporary housing. Alongside the concerns already articulated above is the potential for the identification process to have unintended negative consequences. As McAra and McVie (2010: 189) have argued, there is a danger that the process of identifying children 'at risk' is 'iatrogenic' because categorising individuals as 'at risk' potentially attaches a stigmatising label to them which can have an adverse impact on their self-perception, and potentially their behaviour. Consequently, interventions may serve to exclude further groups that are already excluded.

Tertiary approaches

So far in this chapter we have outlined a range of measures that might be viewed as enhancing 'parental responsibility' in order to promote child wellbeing. This concept was promoted by New Labour but was a recurrent theme in the Thatcher and Major governments (Drakeford, 1996). Tertiary prevention activities continue to emphasise parental responsibility but focus explicitly on the prevention of offending rather than wellbeing in a more general sense; they are preventative in their orientation but can have punitive outcomes. Essentially, they couple 'support' with 'discipline' through the use of sanctions to 'encourage' parents to recognise their responsibilities. The most well known of these is the Parenting Order, described in *Box 7.4*, but these court-directed interventions form part of a broader package of tertiary measures. Parenting Orders, if used correctly, are intended to be a last resort.

- **Parenting programmes** offered by Youth Offending Teams for parents of a child engaged in criminal and/or anti-social behaviour.
- **Parenting contracts**, a less formal agreement with parents of a child engaged in criminal and/or anti-social behaviour. While they claim to be 'voluntary', parents can be subject to a Parenting Order by the courts if they refuse to sign the contract.
- **Fixed Penalty Notices** can also be issued to parents if their child truants (see page 13). At the time of writing they were being piloted in seven police forces for children aged 10–15, which in practice is piloting 'fining' parents for their child's behaviour.

Box 7.4: Parenting Orders

Parenting Orders were introduced in the Crime and Disorder Act 1998. They were rolled out in 2000 and the contexts in which they can be used expanded throughout New Labour's period of office. Their expansion can be attributed, in part, to public support for a seemingly simple solution to a complex problem

(Goldson and Jamieson, 2002). If a child is convicted of an offence or receives another form of court order, usually an ASBO, their parent(s) can be required to attend counselling or guidance sessions on a weekly basis for up three months. This forms part of an order lasting up to 12 months which may have other conditions attached, for example, to ensure a child attends school. They may also be issued when a parent has been convicted of failing to ensure their children attends school (see Chapter Two). If a parent does not comply with the order, they can be taken to court, and non-compliance can lead to a custodial sentence of up to three months and/or a £1,000 fine.

Fierce criticism has accompanied the introduction of the Parenting Order. Most fundamentally, some critical commentators have gone as far as to suggest that Parenting Orders are not compatible with human rights legislation (see, for example, Stone, 2003). Echoing this, others have expressed concern about this intrusion into family life. State intervention appears to have been directed at mothers, leading Holt (2008) to propose that it would be more apt to describe 'Parenting Orders' as 'Mothering Orders'. They have also been used predominantly for parents bringing up children in poor material circumstances, with the aim of transforming their behaviour to middle-class norms divorced from an understanding of the realities of life for poor families (Churchill and Clarke, 2010).

The key question surrounding the parenting initiatives described above is the extent to which parents can be held responsible for the behaviour of their children, especially when the young person is close (in a chronological sense) to becoming an adult. It is likely that by the time they receive formal intervention, and particularly in the case of the Parenting Order, the child's behaviour may be outside of the parents' control (Burney and Gelsthorpe, 2008). The interventions deploy various levers to promote parental compliance: the threat of custody, financial penalties or a more formal intervention (for those not already subject to Parenting Orders). However, for the most disadvantaged parents – and as we have seen, particularly mothers – even the best parenting cannot compensate for exposure to so many risk factors associated with (re)offending. Partly in recognition of this, from 2006 New Labour adopted a 'twin-track' approach, coupling enforcement with intensive support, through the development of Family Intervention Projects (FIPs) (described in **Box 7.5**).

There is also a further question relating to the use of coercion, which particularly concerns the Parenting Order. Mirroring similar debates in the drugs field (see Chapter Six), many have suggested that for parenting initiatives to be effective, families need to enter into them on a voluntary basis (see, for example, Drakeford and Calliva, 2009). There is, however, evidence from the national evaluation of the Youth Justice Board's Parenting Programme that suggests that there were no differences in levels of benefit reported by parents who were referred voluntarily as opposed to being referred via a Parenting Order. Consequently, Holt (2008) has called for a more nuanced understanding which recognises that some parents do find them productive, a finding which has been glossed over in the research literature which has emphasised punitive outcomes (Hodgkinson and Tilley, 2011).This should not be construed as suggesting that coercive approaches should be extended; crucially, we should be asking why it is necessary to get to the stage when children are offending for families to have access to the support they need.

Box 7.5: Family Intervention Projects

Established in 2006, Family Intervention Project (FIPs) work with families who have been described as 'the most challenging' (NatCen, 2009: 1). Funding was made available initially through the *Respect Action Plan* (see page 23), and by December 2011, 159 were in operation at local authority level. Families are referred to these projects by local authorities (housing, social services, anti-social behaviour teams), housing associations and criminal justice agencies. The 'typical' family is white, workless and headed by a lone parent responsible for three or more children aged under 18 (NatCen, 2009, 2011). Support is provided by a 'key worker' who works directly with families and coordinates specialist input from other organisations from the public, private and voluntary sectors. This is usually on an 'outreach' basis in families' own homes but might involve being accommodated in a residential unit. Families are required to sign a 'contract' (known as a Behaviour Support Agreement) that is enforced through sanctions. At the most extreme, these might include termination of a tenancy or children going into 'care'.

FIPs have produced what appear to be impressive outcomes. Of particular interest to readers of this book are the claims made for substantial reductions in crime and/or anti-social behaviour, domestic violence and drug/substance misuse (NatCen, 2011). These have, however, been refuted by Gregg (2010), who describes FIPs as 'a classic case of policy-based evidence' (the subtitle to his report). In a detailed report, he questions both the research evidence that was used to justify the development of FIPs and that collected through an evaluation of their effectiveness. His overall conclusion is that they have not fulfilled their potential to help the poorest and most vulnerable families. Others, as we explore shortly, have expressed similar concerns about mis-targeting in relation to the Troubled Families programme.

'Troubled' or 'troublesome' families?

The Troubled Families programme was formally launched in April 2012 as a targeted intervention for families, which Iain Duncan Smith (2012) described as 'trapped in a twilight world'. It aims to tackle long-standing problems and break the inter-generational cycle of disadvantage. Louise Casey, a somewhat infamous civil servant with a reputation for controversy (see page 30), directs the programme. Local authorities – and specifically Troubled Families coordinators – have been tasked with identifying 'troubled' families, as defined in the introductory paragraph of this chapter. Once families have agreed to participate (and it appears they have little choice but to), the expectation is that they will be assigned to a member of staff (a 'troubleshooter') who will work with them intensively. Detailed definitions of the characteristics of families who will be targeted have been published (see CLG, 2012b) which relate to crime and anti-social behaviour, education and work. There is also scope for local discretion to identify that families might be a cause for concern for other reasons, for example, those with underlying health problems. Families might also be included within the programme because of the criminal or anti-social behaviour of parents or their children or for other crime-related factors, for example, frequent police call-outs or arrests, imprisonment, involvement in gang-related crime or problem drug use.

Embryonic working on the Troubled Families programme predated the August 2011 riots, but these became an important key mechanism for garnering support for it. A further driver was undoubtedly reducing public expenditure. It has been claimed that the most 'troubled' families – estimated to be 120,000 across England – cost the state £9 billion, or £75,000 per family, each year (Duncan Smith, 2012). In comparison with the potential savings, the amount of financial investment in the programme – £448 million over three years (Casey, 2012) – appears to be small. Almost half of the budget (£200 million) is reserved for addressing worklessness (Duncan Smith, 2012). These additional resources are expected to 'incentivise and encourage local authorities and their partners to grasp the nettle' (CLG, 2012b: 1).

The Coalition government has been keen to place 'clear blue water' between this new initiative and programmes launched by the New Labour governments. Launching the programme, Iain Duncan Smith (2012) argued that it was not simply the previous government's approach but rebadged, and he focused on what he perceived to be its distinctive features: cross-departmental coordination to avoid 'siloed government', tackling the root causes rather than treating symptoms and an outcomes-based approach grounded in 'what works'. While some aspects are undoubtedly new, for example, the use of a quasi–PbR funding mechanism comprising of up-front payments or an 'attachment fee' alongside a results-based payment (see CLG, 2012b for more detail, and Chapter Five for a discussion of the use of PbR in other policy areas), its overall distinctiveness has been questioned since it has much in common with the FIPs developed by New Labour.

In the months since the Troubled Families programme was launched, numerous concerns have been raised, which has called into question some of the core principles on which it is based: its commitment to evidence-based policy, the extent to which it is directed at the root causes of family problems and the appropriateness of targeted interventions. We explore each of these issues in turn.

Accompanying the launch of the programme was a report entitled *Listening to families*, written by Casey (2012). Based on 16 interviews with families engaged in FIPs, it did not claim to be an example of 'formal research' (Casey, 2012: 5) or to be representative of the troubled families the government wished to target. Nonetheless, it was suggested that it represented 'a good starting place to inform our thinking and policy development' (Casey, 2012: 5). It was not well received and was described by Professor Ruth Levitas (2012), a leading researcher on poverty and social exclusion, as 'little more than anecdotal tabloid journalism masquerading as research'. The critique is extensive (see Williams, 2012), but essentially the evidence base of the Troubled Families programme was brought into question. Even its claim that there were 120,000 families who met the government's current definition of 'troubled' was challenged by noting that the families originally defined as in need of intensive support were those who fitted a very different definition of 'troubled', defined largely in terms of multiple deprivation rather than with reference to involvement in crime and/or anti-social behaviour (see page 123). Consequently, rather than focusing on the root causes, its core concerns are government priorities, particularly relating to welfare dependency, and it appears to do little to address rising inequalities. Burnett (2012) succinctly describes the final set of concerns as 'ethical questions and moral qualms'. They open up the debate once more about whether targeted provision might have the unintended effect of alienating and stigmatising the very groups they are designed to support.

The extensive critique of the Troubled Families programme has made it difficult to appreciate its positive aspects. Like Parenting Orders, it may be that it has the potential to make a difference to some families, even if it does not turn their lives around. As before, the question about why it is necessary to be defined as 'troubled', or perhaps more appropriately 'troublesome', before benefiting from intervention is a pertinent one.

Summary

- Research on risk and protective factors has repeatedly identified how influential the family is in respect of the likelihood (or not) of an individual in crime and/or anti-social behaviour.
- Over the past 15 years, policy developments have brought the family into the realm of primary, secondary and tertiary crime prevention.
- There is considerable debate over whether targeted prevention activities with 'at risk' families is, on balance, the most appropriate way to reduce (re)offending.
- The terms 'troubled' and 'troublesome' have been conflated and the most intensive forms of support have been targeted at those perceived to be the most 'risky' rather than 'at risk' in a broader sense.

Questions for discussion

- What are the main arguments for and against universal provision, such as Sure Start?
- What are the relative strengths and weaknesses of targeting those perceived to be most at risk of offending; for example, children of prisoners?
- What are the main challenges associated with working with 'troubled' families?
- What are the continuities and points of departure between the approach taken by the New Labour and Coalition governments to family 'support'?

Further reading

- Blyth, M. and Solomon, E. (eds) (2009) *Prevention and youth crime: Is early intervention working?*, Bristol: The Policy Press. This collection of essays, like this chapter, explores critically the assumptions that underpinned New Labour's approach to preventing youth crime.
- Churchill, H. (2011) *Parental rights and responsibilities: Analysing social policy and lived experiences*, Bristol: The Policy Press. Of particular relevance to readers of this chapter is the second part of the book that reviews social policy developments between 1997 and 2010.
- Farrington, D. and Welsh, B. (2007) *Saving children from a life of crime: Early risk factors and effective interventions*, Oxford: Oxford University Press. This book draws on evidence from both the US and the UK on risk and protective factors associated with crime to set out a national early prevention strategy.
- Gregg, D. (2010) *Family Intervention Projects: A classic case of policy-based evidence*, London: Centre for Criminal Justice Studies (www.crimeandjustice.org. uk/opus1786/Family_intervention_projects.pdf). This report reflects critically on the available evidence on FIPs to draw out the negative consequences of such interventions and how they failed to reach their potential.

Guide to electronic resources

- **Action for Children** (www.actionforchildren.org.uk) is a charity that supports and speaks out for the UK's most vulnerable and neglected children and young people. Its project in Dundee was influential in establishing FIPs.
- **Communities and Local Government** (www.communities.gov.uk/communities/troubledfamilies) is the government department with lead responsibility for the Troubled Families programme. Its website explains how the programme works and also includes case studies.
- **Local authorities** are responsible for delivering the Troubled Families programme. Use the list available at www.direct.gov.uk/en/dl1/directories/localcouncils/index.htm to look at what is happening in your area and to compare approaches.
- FIPs are typically run by the voluntary sector. An example of a voluntary sector provider is **Catch22** whose focus is on young people (www.catch-22.org.uk/families).

eight

Governing through crime?
Regulating behaviour in
neoliberal societies

Conclusions to books that focus on different areas of public policy are always challenging to write. Authors wishing to offer more than a summary of previous discussions are faced with the possibility of speculating on the future direction of policy; an ambitious, and some might say, foolhardy task. Books, at least successful ones, have some longevity, and there is always the danger that one's suppositions prove to be far off the mark. As explored in earlier chapters, the messy realities of policy-making and implementation make it difficult to predict with great confidence what policies might be later unveiled since even well-developed policy programmes can fall victim to serendipity. Rather than attempting to reflect with any precision on the future substance of crime control strategies, this chapter adopts a broad-brush approach, and instead draws out the recurring themes from our analysis of crime policy-making in the previous seven chapters. In so doing, we pose a pertinent question: do neoliberal states govern through crime, or are there other mechanisms through which it attempts to regulate the behaviour of its citizens?

We begin by exploring the changing nature of governance, which at its most simplistic refers to the acts of governing: it is what governments do. In neoliberal societies characterised by the growth of marketisation, there has been a shift away from 'Big Government' through a transfer of responsibilities to both civil society and the private sector. The state retains responsibility for its core functions, including crime control, but does not necessarily engage directly in the provision of services. Instead, in some instances it limits its 'hands-on' responsibilities to commissioning services and monitoring contracts with independent providers, essentially overseeing the 'business' of controlling crime which is then conducted by a multiplicity of different agencies from across the public, private and voluntary sector. Increasingly such contracts are offered on a PbR basis so that much of the financial risk is transferred to the contracted provider. Citizens are encouraged to take a more active role in addressing the problem of crime, individually and collectively.

New Labour invested heavily in civic renewal, promising to revitalise civil society. Under New Labour the range of opportunities for the public to volunteer for positions within criminal justice agencies or organisations they worked in partnership with increased substantially as part of a broader agenda of promoting active citizenship. The Coalition government's pursuit of its 'Big Society' agenda, coupled with the emphasis on localism, potentially creates further opportunities for community engagement. This appears to be continuing under the Coalition government, which most recently has announced plans to launch a large-scale informal mentoring scheme for prisoners leaving custody, which will be heavily reliant on public support (see ***Box 4.4***).

The changing nature of governance has required governments to reconstitute social phenomenon as governable problems (O'Malley, 2006). This has frequently involved the redefining of social problems as problems of crime, particularly in countries faced with high crime rates. Based on a detailed and wide-ranging analysis of public policy in the US from the 1960s to the mid-2000s, Simon (2007) argues that the everyday world has became dominated by fear and every citizen treated as a potential criminal. The 'war on crime' provides a new model of governance after expert-guided government policies were met with declining public confidence. It allowed policy-makers to emphasise the vulnerability of citizens by emphasising insecurity. There are parallels here with the work of O'Malley (2004) who argues that risk, alongside uncertainty, is a core neoliberal principle, which forms part of the apparatus of security for governing diverse aspects of social life, including crime. For Simon (2007), the emphasis on insecurity has allowed a new model of governance to be created which has permitted government intervention into all aspects of social life. This, he propounds, has now spilt over into the institutions which govern the everyday life of citizens. By illustration he refers to mandatory drug testing in the workplace, the use of metal detectors to screen school pupils for weapons and the rapid expansion of gated communities. He argues that this predated the 2001 terrorist attacks, but no doubt gave government efforts an added impetus. In essence, he argues that the 'war on crime' has transformed American democracy and created a culture of fear. His thesis complements the early work of Garland (2001) who proposed, based on analysis of both UK and US crime policies, that penal welfarism (with its emphasis on rehabilitation) has been replaced by an exclusionary model of social control. This, he argues, is targeted at the most vulnerable, such as young people, the poor and minority ethnic groups.

The effects of the 'war on crime' are far-reaching since in a sense all members of society become potential criminals. However, the impact is most intense for members of minority ethnic groups, and particularly young males within them, who have been incarcerated in large numbers as the US has pursued its project of 'mass imprisonment'. Highly punitive measures have effectively created a category of 'non-citizens', even among those no longer incarcerated. For example, certain individuals released from prison are not permitted to access financial support in some states following the implementation of the Personal Responsibility and Work Opportunity Act 1996. This federal law prohibits parents (pregnant women excepted) who have been convicted of a drug offence from receiving certain welfare benefits unless they have participated satisfactorily in a drug treatment programme.

Relating Simon's (2007) thesis to the UK, it is not difficult to think of examples of what might be termed the 'criminalisation of social policy'. We can identify a number of social problems that have been redefined as problems of crime; indeed, we have explored a number in this book, such as truancy (see Chapter Two) and drug use (see Chapter Six). We can point to ways in which different areas of social policy have been drawn into the state apparatus to manage crime. A pertinent example is the provision (or not) of welfare benefits (especially out-of-work benefits) as part of the 'toolkit' to tackle the crime problem. This has occurred in two main ways. First, removing the 'right' to particular forms of welfare has been used for citizens who do not fulfil their 'responsibilities' to society. Although never implemented, the removal of welfare benefits from those convicted of involvement in the 2011 riots received both public support in the form of an e-petition (see page 46) and the backing of Iain Duncan Smith (BBC News, 2011). Second, benefits sanctions have been used as a 'lever' to promote compliance with a range of crime control initiatives. They were used briefly as part of a pilot project to improve completion rates for Community Orders (Knight et al, 2004), and were proposed (but not implemented) as a mechanism to increase the number of problem drug users in treatment (Wincup, 2011b).

It is therefore possible to make the claim with some authority that UK citizens have become governed through crime, and certainly anti-social behaviour (Crawford, 2009). However, there is a danger that adopting wholesale the 'governing through crime' thesis over-simplifies the major shifts in policy that have occurred over the past four decades. Referring more specifically to the past decade, we might also argue that the state has 'governed through worklessness' behaviour which is not criminal per se, but which has been identified as criminogenic, and some might argue that it is anti-social. New Labour's aspiration to achieve an ambitious target of 80 per cent employment has resulted in a 'deepening' and 'widening' of the obligation to work, which has intensified under the Coalition government. As part of this strategy, a long list of social 'problems' has been redefined as problems of worklessness and barriers to employability. This permits the state to require individuals who wish to seek its financial support to address them through interventions that are now recast as work-related activities. This project is underpinned by extensive welfare reform (three Acts between 2007 and 2012), and to garner support for these, politicians have tried to appeal to the sentiments of the 'hard-working' public (that is, the 'taxpayer'). In so doing they have made distinctions between those who are 'deserving' and 'undeserving', and exaggerated the extent of benefit fraud and self-selected welfare dependency, contributing to the stigmatisation felt by all benefit claimants (Turn2us, 2012).

Underpinning the projects of governing through crime and worklessness is a desire to activate personal responsibility. Under New Labour, the language of 'rights' and 'responsibilities' began to pervade political discourse, although in other respects it was far from new. This exposes a contradiction within neoliberalism. While the contemporary state has sought to be 'hands off' through the rapid growth of marketisation alongside a project of civil renewal, it has increasingly sought to be 'hands on' through its desire to regulate the behaviour of its citizens. As Wacquant (2009: back cover) argues with reference to the US, neoliberal societies are often characterised in terms of the advent of 'Small Government', but in practice the state is 'overgrown' and 'intrusive'. In the UK contexts, we can see this through successive governments' approaches to address the behaviour of 'irresponsible' citizens. This approach is utilised particularly for individuals who are deemed incapable of acknowledging their responsibilities to society. As a result, 'responsibilisation' strategies are deployed for groups who are too often portrayed as undeserving and dependent non-citizens in need of social discipline. Support is made available to them to change their problematic behaviour(s) but becomes conditional on fulfilling specific obligations. Failure to do so is likely to result in sanctions (criminal or otherwise), which can have the effect of exacerbating further the difficulties that they face.

We have increasingly seen the duties of responsible citizens (for example, to engage in paid work, be a good parent and behave in a pro-social manner) begin to be set out in the form of contracts. Across diverse policy areas such as education, housing and youth justice, contracts have become routinely deployed as a strategy of governance in an attempt to introduce 'regulated self-regulation' (Crawford, 2003: 480). These lay out the responsibilities of citizens to behave in particular ways, promising support for the most 'deserving' cases who, through no fault of their own, need assistance. Enforced through sanctions, these contracts form part of the state apparatus to balance rights and responsibilities. They have both instrumental and ideological functions, representing an attempt to address social problems (and in so doing to reduce public spending) while emphasising the need to bolster individual responsibility and to tackle dependency on the (welfare) state.

As the next General Election edges closer, the desire to appeal to the electorate will become intensified. A challenge for politicians will be to re-engage the public, principally through the media, following on from some of the lowest election figures in peacetime for the winter 2012 Police and Crime Commissioner elections. In such circumstances it is likely that further attempts will be made to be 'tough' on law and order while continuing to pursue a moral welfare agenda. If general election manifestos are translated into real policies, it becomes likely that those whose behaviour appears to pose a threat to dominant political aspirations to 'mend' 'Broken Britain' will be subject to essentially coercive policies for some time to come. Despite the rhetoric of inclusion, such policies are likely to exclude further already excluded groups.

References

ACMD (Advisory Council on the Misuse of Drugs) (2008) *Cannabis: Classification and public health*, London: Home Office.

Advisory Council on the Misuse of Drugs (1998) *Drug misuse and the environment*, London: The Stationery Office.

Allender, P., Brown, G., Bailey, N., Colombo, T., Poole, H. and Saldana, A. (2005) *Prisoner resettlement and housing provision: A good practice ideas guide*, Coventry: Coventry University.

Appleton, C. (2010) *Life after life imprisonment*, Oxford: Oxford University Press.

Atkinson, R. and Helms, G. (eds) (2007) *Securing an urban renaissance: Crime, community and British urban policy*, Bristol: The Policy Press.

Audit Commission (1996) *Misspent youth: Young people and crime*, London: Audit Commission.

Barrett, A. and Harrison, C. (eds) (1999) *Crime and punishment in England: A sourcebook*, London: Routledge.

Barrow Cadbury Trust (2005) *Lost in transition: A report of the Barrow Cadbury Trust Commission on young adults and the criminal justice system*, London: Barrow Cadbury Trust.

Barton, A. (2003) *Illicit drugs: Use and control*, London: Routledge.

Batty, D. (2008) 'Profile: government crime adviser Louise Casey', *The Guardian*, 16 June (www.guardian.co.uk/society/2008/jun/16/justice.prisonsandprobation).

BBC News (2005) 'Visitor rise at "hoodie" ban mall', 19 May (http://news.bbc.co.uk/1/hi/england/kent/4561399.stm).

BBC News (2011) 'England riots: IDS considers ending looters' benefits', 15 August (www.bbc.co.uk/news/uk-14527402).

BBC News (2012) 'Prison gates mentor plan for released inmates', 20 November (www.bbc.co.uk/news/uk-20399401).

Bean, P. (2008) *Drugs and crime* (3rd edn), Cullompton: Willan Publishing.

Bennett, T. and Holloway, K. (2007) *Drug-crime connections*, Cambridge: Cambridge University Press.

Blair, T. (2006) 'Prime Minister's foreword', in *Respect Action Plan*, London: Respect Task Force.

Boaz, A. and Pawson, R. (2005) 'The perilous road from evidence to policy: five journeys compared', *Journal of Social Policy*, 34(2): 175-94.

Bochel, C. and Bochel, H. (2004) *The UK social policy process*, Basingstoke: Palgrave Macmillan.

Bochel, H. (2011) 'Conservative approaches to social policy since 1997', in H. Bochel (ed) *The Conservative Party and social policy*, Bristol: The Policy Press.

Bochel, H. and Defty, A. (2007) 'MPs' attitudes to welfare: a new consensus?', *Journal of Social Policy*, 36(1); 1-17.

Bochel, H. and Defty, A. (2010) 'Power without representation? The House of Lords and social policy', *Social Policy and Society*, 9(3): 367-77.

Bradford, B. (2011) 'Convergence, not divergence? Trends and trajectories in public contact and confidence in the police', *British Journal of Criminology*, 51(1): 179-200.

Braithwaite, J. (2000) 'The new regulatory state and the transformation of criminology', *British Journal of Criminology*, 40(2): 222-38.

Brantingham, P. and Faust, L. (1976) 'A conceptual model of crime prevention', *Crime and Delinquency*, 22(3): 284-96.

Brown, A. (2004) 'Anti-social behaviour, crime control and social control', *Howard Journal of Criminal Justice*, 43(2): 203-11.

Brown, D. (1997) 'PACE ten years on: a review of research', Research Findings No 49, London: Home Office Research and Statistics Directorate.

Bruce, S. and Yearley, S. (2006) *The SAGE dictionary of sociology*, London: Sage Publications.

Burke, L. (2005) *From probation to the National Offender Management Service: Issues of contestability, culture and community involvement*, London: National Association of Probation Officers.

Burnett, R. (2012) 'Early interventions, troubled youth and labelling', *Crime Talk*, 28 June.

Burney, E. (2009) *Making people behave: Anti-social behaviour, politics and policy* (2nd edn), Cullompton: Willan Publishing.

Burney, E. and Gelsthorpe, L. (2008) 'Do we need a "naughty step"? Rethinking the parenting order after ten years', *Howard Journal of Criminal Justice*, 47(5): 470-85.

Butler, I. and Drakeford, M. (2005) *Scandal, social policy and social welfare* (2nd edn), Bristol: The Policy Press.

Cabinet Office (2003) *Trying it out: The role of 'pilots' in policy-making, Report of a review of government pilots*, London: Cabinet Office.

Carnwell, R. and Buchanan, J. (2005a) 'Learning from partnerships: themes and issues', in R. Carnwell and J. Buchanan (eds) *Effective practice in health and social care: A partnership approach*, Buckingham: Open University Press.

Carnwell, R. and Buchanan, J. (eds) (2005b) *Effective practice in health and social care: A partnership approach*, Buckingham: Open University Press.

Carnwell, R. and Carson, A. (2005) 'Understanding partnerships and collaborations', in R. Carnwell and J. Buchanan (eds) *Effective practice in health and social care: A partnership approach*, Buckingham: Open University Press.

Carter, P. (2003) *Managing offenders, changing lives: A new approach*, London: Home Office.

Casey, L. (2012) *Listening to troubled families: A report by Louise Casey*, London: Department for Communities and Local Government.

Cavadino, M. and Dignan, J. (2006) 'Prison privatization', in M. Cavadino and J. Dignan (eds) *Penal systems: A comparative approach*, London: Sage Publications.

Cavadino, M. and Dignan, J. (2007) *The penal system: An introduction* (4th edn), London: Sage Publications.

Cavadino, M., Crow, I. and Dignan, J. (1999) *Criminal justice 2000*, Winchester: Waterside Press.

Cavender, G., Jurik, N. and Cohen, A. (1993) 'The baffling case of the smoking gun: the social ecology of political accounts in the Iran–Contra Affair', *Social Problems*, 40(2): 152-64.

Centre for Social Justice (2006a) *Breakdown Britain: Interim report on the state of the nation* (www.centreforsocialjustice.org.uk/UserStorage/pdf/Pdf%20Exec%20summaries/Breakdown%20Britain.pdf).

Centre for Social Justice (2006b) *Breakthrough Britain, Volume 4: Addictions towards recovery*, London: Centre for Social Justice.

Centre for Social Justice (2012) *It's time to back marriage* (www.centreforsocialjustice.org.uk/publications/its-time-to-back-marriage).

Cheal, D. (2011) 'Family theory', in G. Ritzer and J, Ryan (eds) *The concise encyclopaedia of sociology*, Malden, MA: Wiley-Blackwell.

Christie, N. (2000) *Crime control as industry*, London: Routledge.

Churchill, H. (2012) 'Family support and the Coalition: retrenchment, refocusing and restructuring', in M. Kilkey, G. Ramia and K. Farnsworth (eds) *Social Policy Review 24: Analysis and debate in social policy, 2012*, Bristol: The Policy Press.

Churchill, H. and Clarke, K. (2010) 'Investing in parenting education: a critical review of policy and provision in England', *Social Policy and Society*, 9(1): 39-53.

Civil Service (2010) *Civil Service Code*, www.civilservice.gov.uk/about/values

Clancy, A., Hudson, K., Maguire, M., Peake, R., Raynor, P., Vanstone, M. and Kynch, J. (2006) *Getting out and staying out: Results of the Resettlement Pathfinders*, Bristol: The Policy Press.

Clarke, A., Williams, K., Wydall, S., Gray, P., Liddle, M. and Smith, A. (2011) *Describing and assessing interventions to address anti-social behaviour: Key findings from a study of ASB practice*, Research Report 51: Summary, London: Home Office.

Clarke, K. (2006) 'Childhood, parenting and early intervention: a critical examination of the Sure Start national programme', *Critical Social Policy*, 26(4): 699-721.

Clarke, K. (2010) 'Criminal justice reform', Speech delivered to the Centre for Crime and Justice Studies, 30 June (www.crimlinks.com/News2010/Jun302010c.html).

Clarke, K. (2011) 'Punish the feral rioters, but address our social deficit too', *The Guardian*, 5 September (www.guardian.co.uk/commentisfree/2011/sep/05/punishment-rioters-help).

Clarke, J. and Newman, J. (1997) *The managerial state*, London: Sage Publications.

Clarke, J., Cochrane, A. and McLaughlin, E. (eds) (1994) *Managing social policy*, London: Sage Publications.

Clayton, R. (1992) 'Transitions to drug use: risk and protective factors', in M. Glantz and R. Pickens (eds) *Vulnerability to drug abuse*, Washington, DC: American Psychology Association.

CLG (Communities and Local Government) (2012a) *Rough sleeping statistics England: Autumn 2011, Experimental statistics*, London: CLG.

CLG (2012b) *The Troubled Families Programme: Financial framework for the Troubled Families Programme's payment-by-results schemes for local authorities*, London: CLG.

Clinks (2011) *Clinks response to the Ministry of Justice's Green Paper 'Breaking the cycle: Effective punishment, sentencing and rehabilitation of offenders'* (www.clinks.org/assets/files/PDFs/Clinks%20repsonse%20to%20Breaking%20the%20Cycle.pdf).

Cohen, S. (1979) 'The punitive city: notes on the dispersal of social control', *Contemporary Crises*, 3: 339-63.

Cole, A., Galbraith, I., Lyon, P. and Ross, H. (2007) 'PS Plus: a prison (lately) probation–based employment resettlement model', in A. Hucklesby and L. Hagley-Dickinson (eds) *Prisoner resettlement: Policy and practice*, Cullompton: Willan Publishing.

Collins, J. (2012) Contribution to 'The big debate: police and crime commissioners: will directly elected police and crime commissioners give a greater say to the public over policing issues or politicise the delivery of police services?', *The Guardian*, 16 April (www.guardian.co.uk/public-leaders-network/2012/apr/16/big-debate-police-crime-commissioners).

Collins, N. (2010) 'Labour invents 33 new crimes every month', *The Telegraph*, 23 January (www.telegraph.co.uk/news/politics/labour/7050044/Labour-invents-33-new-crimes-every-month.html#).

Conservative Party (2010) *Big society, not big government*, London: Conservative Party.

Cook, D. (2006) *Criminal and social justice*, London: Sage Publications.

Cooper, Y. (2011) Speech to the Police Federation Conference, 17 May (www.labour.org.uk/cooper-speech-police-federation-conference,2011-05-17).

Corston, J. (2007) *The Corston Report: A report by Baroness Jean Corston of a review of women with particular vulnerabilities in the criminal justice system*, London: Home Office.

Crawford, A. (1998) *Crime prevention and community safety: Politics, policies and practices*, London: Longman.

Crawford, A. (2003) 'Contractual governance of deviant behaviour', *Journal of Law and Society*, 30(4): 479-505.

Crawford, A. (2009) 'Governing through anti-social behaviour: regulatory challenges to criminal justice', *British Journal of Criminology*, 49(6): 810-31.

Crawford, A. and Lister, S. (2007) *The use and impact of Dispersal Orders*, York: Joseph Rowntree Foundation (www.jrf.org.uk/publications/use-and-impact-dispersal-orders).

Crawford, A., Lister, S., Blackburn, S. and Burnett, J. (2005) *Plural policing: The mixed economy of visible patrols in England and Wales*, Bristol: The Policy Press.

Crawley, E. (2004) 'Resettlement and the older prisoner', *Criminal Justice Matters*, 56: 32-33.

Crawley, E. and Sparks, R. (2006) 'Is there life after imprisonment? How elderly men talk about imprisonment and release', *Criminology and Criminal Justice*, 6(1): 63-82.

Criminal Justice Inspection Northern Ireland (2011) *An inspection of prisoner resettlement by the Northern Ireland Prison Service*, Belfast: Criminal Justice Inspection Northern Ireland.

Croall, H., Mooney, G. and Munro, M. (2010) *Criminal justice in Scotland*, Cullompton: Willan Publishing.

Crowther-Dowey, C. (2007) 'The police and drugs', in M. Simpson, T. Shildrick and R. MacDonald (eds) *Drugs in Britain: Supply, consumption and control*, Basingstoke: Palgrave Macmillan.

Curtis, J. and Seyd, B. (2012) 'Will the coalition's constitutional reforms re-engage a sceptical electorate?' (www.natcen.ac.uk/media/844497/bsa-29-research-findings.pdf).

Deacon, A. and Patrick, R. (2011) 'A new welfare settlement? The Coalition government and welfare-to-work', in H. Bochel (ed) *The Conservative Party and social policy*, Bristol: The Policy Press.

Dean, H. (2006) *Social policy*, Cambridge: Polity Press.

DCSF (Department for Children, Schools and Families) (2009) *Think Family Toolkit* (www.education.gov.uk/publications/eOrderingDownload/Think-Family.pdf).

DeKeseredy, W. (2011) *Contemporary critical criminology*, London: Routledge.

DfES (Department for Education and Skills) (2003) *Every Child Matters*, London: DfES.

Disley, E., Rubin, J., Scragg, E., Burrowes, N. and Culley, D. (2011) *Lessons learned from the planning and early implementation of the Social Impact Bond at HMP Peterborough*, Research Series 5/11, London: Ministry of Justice.

Dodgson, K., Goodwin, P., Howard, P., Llewellyn-Thomas, S., Mortimer, E., Russell, N. and Weiner, M. (2001) *Electronic monitoring of released prisoners: An evaluation of the Home Detention Curfew Scheme*, Home Office Research Study 222, London: Home Office.

Dolowitz, D. (2000) 'Policy transfer: a new framework for analysis', in D. Dolowitz (ed) *Policy transfer and British social policy*, Buckingham: Open University Press.

Dolowitz, D. and Marsh, D. (1996) 'Who learns what from whom: a review of the policy transfer literature', *Political Studies*, 44(2): 343-57.

Donoghue, J. (2010) *Anti-social Behaviour Orders: A culture of control?*, Basingstoke: Palgrave Macmillan.

Downes, D. and Morgan, R. (2007) 'No turning back: the politics of law and order into the millennium', in M. Maguire, R. Morgan and R. Reiner (eds) *The Oxford handbook of criminology* (4th edn), Oxford: Oxford University Press.

Downes, D. and Morgan, R. (2012) 'Overtaking on the Left? The politics of "law and order" in the "Big Society"', in M. Maguire, R. Morgan and R. Reiner (eds) *The Oxford handbook of criminology* (5th edn), Oxford: Oxford University Press.

Drakeford, M. (1996) 'Parents of young people in trouble', *The Howard Journal of Criminal Justice*, 35(3): 242-55.

Drakeford, M. and Butler, I. (2007) 'Everyday tragedies: justice, scandal and young people in contemporary Britain', *The Howard Journal of Criminal Justice*, 46(3): 219-35.

Drakeford, M. and Calliva, K. (2009) 'Working with parents in the youth justice system: compulsory help and "doing good"', *Practice*, 21(4): 215-27.

DrugScope (2010) 'Cocaine and crack' (www.drugscope.org.uk/resources/drugsearch/drugsearchpages/cocaineandcrack).

Duke, K. (2010) 'The focus on crime and coercion in UK drug policy', in S. MacGregor (ed) *Responding to drug misuse: Research and policy priorities in health and social care*, London: Routledge.

Duke, K. (2013) 'From crime to recovery: the reframing of British Drugs Policy?', *Journal of Drug Issues*, 43(1): 39-55.

Duke, L. and MacGregor, S. (1997) *Tackling drugs locally: The implementation of Drug Action Teams in England* (with K. Duke), London: Home Office.

Duncan Smith, I. (2012) 'Troubled families', Speech to the 4Children's 2012 Annual Children and Families Policy Conference, London, 25 April (www.dwp.gov.uk/newsroom/ministers-speeches/2012/25-04-12.shtml).

DWP (Department for Work and Pensions) (2010) *Universal Credit: Welfare that works*, London: DWP.

DWP (2011) *The Work Programme*, London: DWP.

DWP (2012) 'Government launches employment support for prisoners', DWP Press release, 6 March (www.dwp.gov.uk/newsroom/press-releases/2012/mar-2012/dwp021-12.shtml).

Eisenstadt, N. (2002) 'Sure Start: key principles and ethos', *Child: Care, Health and Development*, 28(1): 3-4.

Elliott, C. and Quinn, F. (2010) *The English legal system* (12th edn), London: Longman.

Ellison, G. and O'Mahoney, D. (2010) 'Crime and criminal justice in Northern Ireland', in G. Newman (ed) *Crime and punishment across the world*, Santa Barbara, CA: ABC-CLIO.

Farrall, S. and Calverley, A. (2005) *Understanding desistance from crime: Emerging theoretical directions in resettlement and rehabilitation*, Buckingham: Open University Press.

Farrall, S. and Hay, C. (2010) 'Not so tough on crime? Why weren't the Thatcher governments more radical in reforming the criminal justice system?', *British Journal of Criminology*, 50(3): 550-69.

Farrington, D. (2007) 'Childhood risk factors and risk-focused prevention', in M. Maguire, R. Reiner and R. Morgan (eds) *The Oxford handbook of criminology* (3rd edn), Oxford: Oxford University Press.

Faulkner, D. (2001) *Crime, state and the citizen*, Hook: Waterside Press.

Faulkner, D. (2004) 'Why officials must make their voices heard', *The Guardian*, 22 December.

Faulkner, D. (2011) 'Criminal justice reform at a time of austerity: what needs to be done', in A. Silvestri (ed) *Lessons for the Coalition: An end of term report on New Labour and criminal justice*, London: Centre for Crime and Justice Studies.

Faulkner, D. and Burnett, R. (2011) *Where next for criminal justice?*, Bristol: The Policy Press.

Fionda, J. (2005) *Devils and angels: Youth policy and crime*, Oxford: Hart Publishing.

Fitzpatrick, T. (2011) *Understanding the environment and social policy*, Bristol: The Policy Press.

Fletcher, D., Taylor, A., Hughes, S. and Breeze, J. (2001) *Recruiting and employing offenders: The impact of the Police Act*, York: Joseph Rowntree Foundation (www.jrf.org.uk/publications/recruiting-and-employing-offenders-impact-police-act).

Foster, J. (2000) 'Social exclusion, crime and drugs', *Drugs: Education, Prevention and Policy*, 7(4): 317-30.

Fox, C. and Albertson, K. (2011) 'Payment by Results and Social Impact Bonds', *Criminology and Criminal Justice*, 11(5): 395-413.

Friendship, C., Beech, A. and Browne, K. (2002) 'Reconviction as an outcome measure in research. A methodological note', *British Journal of Criminology*, 42(2): 442-44.

Garland, D. (1985) *Punishment and welfare: A history of penal strategies*, Aldershot: Gower.

Garland, D. (2001) *A culture of control: Crime and social order in contemporary society*, Oxford: Oxford University Press.

Garside, R. (2004) *Crime, persistent offenders and the justice gap*, London: The Crime and Society Foundation (www.crimeandjustice.org.uk/opus283/DP1Oct04.pdf).

Gatrell, V. (1990) 'Crime, authority and the policeman-state', Extract reproduced in J. Muncie, E. McLaughlin and M. Langan (eds) (1996) *Criminological perspectives: A reader*, London: Sage Publications.

Gelsthorpe, L. and Sharpe, G. (2007) 'Women and resettlement', in A. Hucklesby and L. Hagley-Dickinson (eds) *Prisoner resettlement: Policy and practice*, Cullompton: Willan Publishing.

Ghate, D. and Ramella, M. (2002) *Positive parenting: The National Evaluation of the Youth Justice Board's Parenting Programme*, London: Youth Justice Board.

Giddens, A. (1990) *The consequences of modernity*, Cambridge: Polity Press.

Glass, N. (1999) 'Sure Start: the development of an early intervention programme for young children in the United Kingdom', *Children and Society*, 13: 257-64.

Goldson, B. and Jamieson, J. (2002) 'Youth crime, the "parenting deficit" and state intervention: a contextual critique', *Youth Justice*, 2(2): 82-9.

Goodey, J. (2005) *Victims and victimology: Research, policy and practice*, Harrow: Pearson Longman.

Gossop, M. (2005) *Treatment outcomes: What we know and what we need to know*, London: National Treatment Agency for Substance Misuse.

Gough, D. (2012) 'Revolution, marketisation: the penal system and the voluntary sector', in A. Silvestri (ed) *Critical reflections: Social and criminal justice in the first year of the Coalition government*, London: Centre for Criminal Justice Studies.

Graham, P. and Clarke, J. (2001) 'Dangerous places: crime and the city', in J. Muncie and E. McLaughlin (eds) *The problem of crime* (2nd edn), London: Sage Publications.

Greer, C. (2009) 'Crime and media: understanding the connections', in C. Hale, K. Hayward, A. Wahidin and E. Wincup (eds) *Criminology* (2nd edn), Oxford: Oxford University Press.

Greer, C. and Reiner, R. (2012) 'Mediated mayhem: media, crime, criminal justice', in M. Maguire, R. Morgan and R. Reiner (eds) *The Oxford handbook of criminology* (5th edn), Oxford: Oxford University Press.

Gregg, D. (2010) *Family Intervention Projects: A classic case of policy-based evidence*, London: Centre for Criminal Justice Studies.

Grover, C. (2008) *Crime and inequality*, Cullompton: Willan Publishing.

Gyngell, K. (2011) *Breaking the habit: Why the state should stop dealing drugs and start doing rehab*, London: Centre for Policy Studies.

Hadfield, P., Lister, S. and Traynor, P. (2009) '"This town's a different town today": policing and regulating the night-time economy', *Criminology and Criminal Justice*, 9(4): 465-85.

Hagell, A. (2004) *Key elements of effective practice: Resettlement*, London: Youth Justice Board.

Hale, C. and Fitzgerald, M. (2009) 'The politics of law and order', in C. Hale, K. Hayward, A. Wahidin and E. Wincup (eds) *Criminology* (2nd edn), Oxford: Oxford University Press.

Hammersley, M. (1995) *The politics of social research*, London: Sage Publications.

Hancock, L. (2004) 'Criminal justice, public opinion, fear and popular politics', in J. Muncie and D. Wilson (eds) *The student handbook of criminology and criminal justice*, London: Cavendish Publishing.

Harm Reduction International (2010) *Briefing 4 human rights and drug policy: Compulsory drug treatment* (www.ihra.net/files/2010/11/01/IHRA_BriefingNew_4.pdf).

Harlow, C. (1981) 'Report of the Royal Commission on Criminal Procedure', *The Political Quarterly*, vol 52, no 2, pp 239-43.

Hartfree, Y., Dearden, C. and Pound, E. (2008) *Supporting ex-prisoners in their lives after prison*, Research Report No 509, London: Department for Work and Pensions.

Hay, G., Gannon, M., Casey, J. and Millar, T. (2011) *National and regional estimates of the prevalence of opiate and/or crack cocaine use 2009/106: A summary of key findings*, London: National Treatment Agency for Substance Misuse.

Hayward, K. (2004) *City limits: Crime, consumer culture and the urban experience*, London: Cavendish Publishing.

Hazel, N. (2004) 'Resettlement of young offenders: can practice make perfect?', *Criminal Justice Matters*, 56: 30-1.

Heaven, O. and Hudson, B. (2005) '"Race", ethnicity and crime', in C. Hale, K. Hayward, A. Wahidin and E. Wincup (eds) *Criminology*, Oxford: Oxford University Press.

Hedderman, C. (2007) 'Rediscovering resettlement: narrowing the gap between policy rhetoric and practice reality', in A. Hucklesby and L. Hagley-Dickinson (eds) *Prisoner resettlement: Policy and practice*, Cullompton: Willan Publishing.

Heidensohn, F. and Silvestri, M. (2012) 'Gender and crime', in M. Maguire, R. Morgan and R. Reiner (eds) *The Oxford handbook of criminology* (5th edn), Oxford: Oxford University Press.

Hillyard, P. and Tombs, S. (2008) 'Beyond criminology?', in D. Dorling, D. Gordon, P. Hillyard, C. Pantazis, S. Pemberton and S. Tombs (eds) *Criminal obsessions: Why harm matters more than crime* (2nd edn), London: Centre for Crime and Justice Studies.

Hinsliff, B., Weitz, K. and Bright, M. (2005) 'Fashion item or symbol of fear? A moral debate sparked by a shopping mall's ban on hooded tops goes right to the heart of British life', *The Observer*, 15 May (www.guardian.co.uk/society/2005/may/15/youthjustice.politics).

HM Government (2008) *Drugs: Protecting families and communities. The 2008 drug strategy*, London: HM Government.

HM Government (2010a) *The Coalition: Our programme for government*, London: Cabinet Office.

HM Government (2010b) *Drug strategy 2010: Reducing demand, restricting supply and building recovery: Supporting people to live a drug free life*, London: HM Government.

HM Government (2012) *Open public services 2012*, London: Cabinet Office.

HM Inspectorates of Prisons and Probation (2001) *Through the prison gate: A joint thematic review by HM Inspectorates of Prisons and Probation*, London: Home Office.

Hodgkinson, S. and Tilley, N. (2011) 'Tackling anti-social behaviour: lessons from New Labour for the Coalition government', *Criminology and Criminal Justice*, 11(4): 283-305.

Holt, A. (2008) 'Room for resistance? Parenting orders, disciplinary power and the construction of the bad parent', in P. Squires (ed) *ASBO nation: The criminalisation of nuisance*, Bristol: The Policy Press.

Home Affairs Committee (2011) *New landscape of policing*, 14th Report, London: House of Commons.

Home Affairs Committee (2012) *Drugs: Breaking the cycle*, London: The Stationery Office.

Homel, P., Nutley, S., Webb, B. and Tilley, N. (2004) *Investing to deliver: Reviewing the implementation of the UK Crime Reduction Programme*, Home Office Research Study 281, London: Home Office.

Home Office (1984) *Probation Service in England and Wales: Statement of national objectives and priorities*, London: Home Office.

Home Office (1985) *Tackling drug misuse: A summary of the government's strategy*, London: Home Office.

Home Office (1988) *National standards for Community Service Orders*, London: Home Office.

Home Office (1992) *National standards for the supervision of offenders in the community*, London: Home Office

Home Office (1995) *Tackling drugs together: A strategy for England 1995-1998*, London: Home Office.

Home Office (1998a) *Crime and Disorder Act 1998: Introductory guide*, London: Home Office.

Home Office (1998b) *Joining forces to protect the public: Prison-probation*, London: Home Office. Home Office (2002) *Updated drug strategy 2002*, London: Home Office.

Home Office (2004a) *Defining and measuring anti-social behaviour*, Development and Practice Report 26, London: Home Office.

Home Office (2004b) *Reducing reoffending: National action plan*, London: Home Office.

Home Office (2010) *Policing in the 21st century: Reconnecting police and the people*, London: Home Office.

Home Office (2011a) *Rebalancing the Licensing Act: A consultation on empowering individuals, families and local communities to shape and determine local licensing*, London: Home Office.

Home Office (2011b) *More effective responses to anti-social behaviour*, London: Home Office.

Home Office (2012a) *Integrated offender management* (www.homeoffice.gov. uk/crime/reducing-reoffending/iom/).

Home Office (2012b) *Drug misuse declared: Findings from the 2011/12 Crime Survey for England and Wales*, London: Home Office.

Hope, C. (2010) 'Middle classes told to stop using Sure Start: "Sharp-elbowed" middle class families should stop accessing state-supported child care, David Cameron said yesterday', *The Telegraph*, 11 August (www.telegraph.co.uk/news/politics/david-cameron/7937248/Middle-classes-told-to-stop-using-Sure-Start.html).

Hope, C. (2011) 'Prison doesn't achieve anything, says Ken Clarke', *The Telegraph*, 16 October (www.telegraph.co.uk/news/uknews/law-and-order/8768492/Prison-doesnt-achieve-anything-says-Ken-Clarke.html).

Hope, T. and Walters, R. (2008) *Critical thinking about the use of research*, London: Centre for Crime and Justice Studies.

Hopkins Burke, R. (2009) *An introduction to criminological theory* (3rd edn), Cullompton: Willan Publishing.

Hough, M. (2011) 'Crime and criminal justice', in H. Bochel (ed) *The Conservative Party and social policy*, Bristol: The Policy Press.

Hough, M. and Roberts, J. (2004) *Youth crime and youth justice: Public opinion in England and Wales*, Bristol: The Policy Press.

Hough, M., Allen, R. and Padel, U. (eds) (2006) *Reshaping probation and prisons: The New Offender Management Framework*, Bristol: The Policy Press.

House of Commons (2006) *Report of the Zahid Mubarek Inquiry*, London: The Stationery Office.

House of Common Select Committee (2011) 'E-petition debate on response to riots', 13 October (www.parliament.uk/business/committees/committees-a-z/commons-select/backbench-business-committee/news/e-petition-debate-on-response-to-riots/).

House of Lords/House of Commons (2012) *Joint Committee Report on the draft House of Lords Reform Bill – First report*, London: The Stationery Office (www.publications.parliament.uk/pa/jt201012/jtselect/jtdraftref/284/28402.htm).

Howard, P. (2006) *Offender assessment system: An evaluation of the second pilot*, Findings No 278, London: Home Office.

Howe, G. (2007) 'If it isn't broke …', contribution to N. Baldwin, 'The House of Lords – Into the future', *Journal of Legislative Studies*, 13(2): 197-209.

Hucklesby, A. and Hagley-Dickinson, L. (eds) (2007a) *Prisoner resettlement: Policy and practice*, Cullompton: Willan Publishing.

Hucklesby, A. and Hagley-Dickinson, L. (2007b) 'Introduction', in A. Hucklesby and L. Hagley-Dickinson (eds) *Prisoner resettlement: Policy and practice*, Cullompton: Willan Publishing.

Hucklesby, A. and Wincup, E. (eds) (2010) *Drug interventions and criminal justice*, Buckingham: Open University Press.

Hucklesby, A. and Worrall, J. (2007) 'The voluntary sector and prisoners' resettlement', in A. Hucklesby and L. Hagley-Dickinson (eds) *Prisoner resettlement: Policy and practice*, Cullompton: Willan Publishing.

Hudson, J. and Lowe, S. (2009) *Understanding the policy process: Analysing welfare policy and practice* (2nd edn), Bristol: The Policy Press.

Hudson, K. (2007) 'The SWing model of resettlement: some reflections', in A. Hucklesby and L. Hagley-Dickinson (eds) *Prisoner resettlement: Policy and practice*, Cullompton: Willan Publishing.

Hughes, C. and Stevens, A. (2010) 'What can we learn from the Portuguese decriminalization of illicit drugs?', *British Journal of Criminology*, 50(6): 999-1022.

Hughes, G. and Rowe, M. (2007) 'Neighbourhood policing and community safety: researching the instabilities of the local governance of crime, disorder and security in contemporary UK', *Criminology and Criminal Justice*, 7(4): 317-46.

Innes, J. (2011) 'Public perceptions', in R. Chaplin, J. Flatley and K. Smith (eds) *Crime in England and Wales 2010/11: Findings from the British Crime Survey and police recorded crime* (2nd edn), London: Home Office.

International Centre for Prison Studies (2012) *Entire world – Prison population rates per 100,000 of the national population* (www.prisonstudies. org/info/worldbrief/wpb_stats.php?area=all&category=wb_poprate).

Ipsos MORI (2008) *Drugs: Our community, your say: A report on the 2008 Drug Strategy Consultation: Views on reclassifying cannabis to a Class B drug*, London: Ipsos MORI.

Jackson, M. (2011) 'MPs "ignore" riots e-petition in Westminster debate', BBC News, 11 October (www.bbc.co.uk/news/uk-politics-15283837).

Janowitz, M. (1972) *Sociological models and social policy*, Morriston, NJ: General Learning Systems.

Jewkes, Y. (2010) *Media and crime* (2nd edn), London: Sage Publications.

Johnsen, S. and Fitzpatrick, S. (2007) *The impact of enforcement on street users*, York: Joseph Rowntree Foundation (www.jrf.org.uk/publications/ impact-enforcement-street-users-england).

Jones, A., Donmall, M., Millar, T., Dollin, L., Anderson, T., Gittins, M., Abeywardana, V. and D'Souza, J. (2009) *The Drug Treatment Outcomes Research Study: Final outcomes report*, London: Home Office.

Jones, T. (2009) 'Policing', in C. Hale, K. Hayward. A. Wahidin and E. Wincup (eds) *Criminology*, 2nd edn, Oxford: Oxford University Press.

Jones, T. and Newburn, T. (1996) *Private security and public policing*, Oxford: Oxford University Press.

Jones, T. and Newburn, T. (2002a) 'Policy convergence and control in the USA and the UK: Streams of influence and levels of impact', *Criminal Justice*, 2(2): 173-203.

Jones, T. and Newburn, T. (2002b) 'Learning from Uncle Sam? Exploring US influences on British crime control policy', *Governance*, 15(1): 97-119.

Jones, T. and Newburn, T. (2007) *Policy transfer and criminal justice: Explaining US influence over British crime control policy*, Buckingham: Open University Press.

Joseph Rowntree Foundation (2012) *Child poverty in the UK* (www.jrf. org.uk/work/workarea/child-poverty).

Kemshall, H. (2007) 'Dangerous offenders: release and resettlement', in A. Hucklesby and L. Hagley-Dickinson (eds) *Prisoner resettlement: Policy and practice*, Cullompton: Willan Publishing.

Kemshall, H. and Hilder, S. (2012) 'Multi-agency approaches to effective risk management in the community in England and Wales', in L. Craig, L. Dixon and T. Gannon (eds) *What works in offender rehabilitation: An evidence-based approach to assessment and treatment*, Oxford: Wiley-Blackwell.

Kinsella, B. (2011) *Tackling knife crime together: A review of local anti-knife crime projects*, London: Home Office.

Kirton, D. (2009) 'Young people and crime', in C. Hale, K. Hayward, A. Wahidin and E. Wincup (eds) *Criminology* (2nd edn), Oxford: Oxford University Press.

Knepper, P. (2007) *Criminology and social policy*, London: Sage Publications.

Knight, T., Mowlam, A., Woodfield, K., Lewis, J., Purdon, S. and Kitchen, S. with Roberts, C. (2004) *Evaluation of the community sentences and withdrawal of benefits pilots*, Research Report No 198, London: Department for Work and Pensions.

Lacey, N. (1994a) 'Government as manager, citizen and consumer: the case of the Criminal Justice Act 1991', *Modern Law Review*, 57(4): 534-54.

Lacey, N. (1994b) 'Missing the wood . . . pragmatism and theory in the Royal Commission', in M. McConville and L. Bridges (eds) *Criminal justice in crisis*, London: Edward Elgar.

Leach, R., Coxall, B. and Robins, L. (2011) *British politics*, Basingstoke: Palgrave Macmillan.

Levitas, R. (2012) *Still not listening* (www.poverty.ac.uk/articles-families/still-not-listening).

Levitas, R., Pantazis, C., Fahmy, E., Gordon, D., Lloyd, E. and Patsios, D. (2007) *The multi-dimensional analysis of social exclusion*, London: Cabinet Office.

Lewis, P., Newburn, T., Taylor, M. and Ball, J. (2011) 'Rioters say anger with police fuelled summer unrest', *The Guardian*, 5 December (www.guardian.co.uk/uk/2011/dec/05/anger-police-fuelled-riots-study).

Lewis, S., Maguire, M., Raynor, P., Vanstone, M. and Vennard, J. (2007) 'What works in resettlement? Findings from seven Pathfinders for short-term prisoners in England and Wales', *Criminology and Criminal Justice*, 7(1): 33–53.

Lewis, S., Vennard, J., Maguire, M., Raynor, P., Vanstone, M., Raybould, S. and Rix, A. (2003) *The resettlement of short-term prisoners: An evaluation of seven pathfinders*, RDS Occasional Paper No 83, London: Home Office.

Liddle, M. and Gelsthorpe, L. (1994) *Inter-agency crime prevention: Organising local delivery*, Crime Prevention Unit Series Paper 52, London: Home Office.

Lipsky, M. (1980) *Street-level bureaucracy*, New York: Russell Sage Foundation.

Lister, S., Seddon, T., Wincup, E., Barrett, S. and Traynor, P. (2008) *Street policing of problem drug users*, York: Joseph Rowntree Foundation.

Lloyd, C., Mair, G. and Hough, M. (1994) *Explaining reconviction rates: A critical analysis*, Home Office Research Study No 136, London: Home Office.

Lund, B. (2011) *Understanding housing policy* (2nd edn), Bristol: The Policy Press.

MacGregor, S. (2010) 'Policy responses to the drug problem', in S. MacGregor (ed) *Responding to drug misuse: Research and policy priorities in health and social care*, London: Routledge.

MacIntyre, D. (1993) 'Major pulls party back to basics: prime minister emphasises need for unity and says any infighting must be keep behind closed doors', *The Independent*, 9 October (www.independent.co.uk/news/major-pulls-party-back-to-basics-prime-minister-emphasises-need-for-unity-and-says-any-infighting-must-be-kept-behind-closed-doors-1509581.html).

Mackenzie, S., Bannister, J., Flint, J., Parr, S., Millie, A. and Fleetwood, J. (2010) *The drivers of perceptions of anti-social behaviour*, Research Report 34: Key Implications, London: Home Office (www.homeoffice.gov.uk/publications/science-research-statistics/research-statistics/crime-research/horr34/horr34-key-implications?view=Binary).

Macpherson, W. (1999) *The Stephen Lawrence Inquiry: Report of an inquiry by Sir William Macpherson on Cluny*, London: The Stationery Office.

McAra, L. (2004) *Truancy, school exclusion and substance misuse*, Number 4, The Edinburgh Study of Youth Transitions and Crime (www.law.ed.ac.uk/cls/esytc/findings/digest4.pdf).

McAra, L. (2005) 'Negotiated order, gender, youth transition and crime', Selected papers from the 2003 British Criminology Conference, Bangor, 6 June (www.britsoccrim.org/volume6/005.pdf).

McAra, L. and McVie, S. (2010) 'Youth crime and justice: key messages from the "Edinburgh Study of Youth Transitions and Crime"', *Criminology and Criminal Justice*, 10(2): 179-209.

McIvor, G., Trotter, C. and Sheehan, R. (2009) 'Women, resettlement and desistance', *Probation Journal*, 56(4): 347-61.

McKeganey, N. (2011) *Controversies in drugs policy and practice*, Basingstoke: Palgrave Macmillan.

McLaughlin, E. (2006) 'Managerialsm' in E. McLaughlin and J. Muncie (eds) *The SAGE Dictionary of Criminology*, 2nd edn, London: Sage.

McLaughlin, E., Muncie, J. and Hughes, G. (2001) 'The permanent revolution: New Labour, new public management and the modernization of criminal justice', *Criminal Justice*, 1(3): 301-18.

Maguire, M. (2004) 'The Crime Reduction Programme in England and Wales: reflections on the vision and reality', *Criminal Justice*, 4(3): 213-37.

Maguire, M. (2023) 'The voluntary sector and criminal justice', *Criminology and Criminal Justice*, 12(5): 483-505.

Maguire, M. and Nolan, J. (2007) 'Accommodation and related services for ex-prisoners', in A. Hucklesby and L. Hagley-Dickinson (eds) *Prisoner resettlement: Policy and practice*, Cullompton: Willan Publishing.

Maguire, M. and Norris, C. (1993) *The Conduct and Supervision of Criminal Investigations*, The Royal Commission on Criminal Justice, Research Study No 5, London: HMSO.

Maguire, M. and Raynor, P. (1997) 'The revival of throughcare: rhetoric and reality in automatic conditional release', *British Journal of Criminology*, 37(1): 1-14.

Maguire, M. and Raynor, P. (2006) 'How the resettlement of prisoners promotes desistance from crime: or does it?', *Criminology and Criminal Justice*, 6(1): 19-38.

Maguire, M., Kemshall, H., Noaks, L. and Wincup, E. (2001) *Risk management of sexual and violent offenders: The work of Public Protection Panels*, Police Research Series Paper 139, London: Home Office.

Maguire, M., Raynor, P., Vanstone, M. and Kynch, J. (2000) 'Voluntary aftercare and the probation service: a case of diminishing responsibility', *Howard Journal of Criminal Justice*, 39(3): 234-48.

Maguire, M., Holloway, K., Liddle, M., Gordon, F., Gray, P., Smith, A. and Wright, S. (2010) *Evaluation of the Transitional Support Scheme*, Cardiff: Welsh Assembly Government.

Mair, G. (2005) 'Electronic monitoring in England and Wales: evidence-based or not?', *Criminal Justice*, 5(3): 257-77.

Mair, G. and Burke, L. (2011) *Redemption, rehabilitation and risk management: A history of probation*, London: Routledge.

Mair, G. and Millings, M. (2010) 'Arrest referral and drug testing', in A. Hucklesby and E. Wincup (eds) *Drug interventions in criminal justice*, Buckingham: Open University Press.

Mair, G. and Nee, C. (1990) *Electronic monitoring: The trials and their results*, Home Office Research Study 120, London: Home Office.

Mair, G., Lloyd, C. and Hough, M. (1997) 'The limitations of reconviction rates', in G. Mair (ed) *Evaluating the effectiveness of community penalties*, Aldershot: Ashgate.

Maruna, S. and LeBel, T. (2002) 'Revisiting ex-prisoner re-entry: a new buzzword in search of a narrative', in S. Rex and M. Tonry (eds) *Reform and punishment: The future of sentencing*, Cullompton: Willan Publishing,

Matthews, R. and Pitts, J. (eds) (2001) *Crime, disorder and community safety*, London: Routledge.

Mawby, R. and Worrall, A. (2011) *Probation workers and their occupational cultures*, Leicester: University of Leicester (www2.le.ac.uk/departments/ criminology/documents/Final_report_Nov_2011%20-17%20Nov%20 2011.pdf).

May, C. (1999) *Explaining reconviction following a community sentence: The role of social factors*, Home Office Research Study 192, London: Home Office.

May, C., Warburton, H., Turnbull, P. and Hough, M. (2002) *Times they are a-changing: The policing of cannabis*, York: Joseph Rowntree Foundation.

May, J., Cloke, P. and Johnsen, S. (2005) 'Re-phasing neo-liberalism: New Labour and Britain's crisis of street homelessness', *Antipode*, 37(4): 703-30.

May, T., Duffy, M., Warburton, H. and Hough, M. (2007) *Policing cannabis as a class C drug: An arresting change?*, York: Joseph Rowntree Foundation.

Measham, F. and South, N. (2012) 'Drugs, alcohol and crime', in M. Maguire, R. Morgan and R. Reiner (eds) *The Oxford handbook of criminology* (5th edn), Oxford: Oxford University Press.

Mentoring and Befriending Foundation (2012) *What is mentoring and befriending?* (www.mandbf.org/guidance-and-support/what-is-mentoring-and-befriending).

Metcalf, H., Anderson, T. and Rolfe, H. (2001) *Barriers to employment for offenders and ex-offenders – Part one: Barriers to employment for offenders and ex-offenders*, Research Report No 155, London: Department for Work and Pensions (http://research.dwp.gov.uk/asd/asd5/report_abstracts/ rr_abstracts/rra_155.asp).

Mills, H. and Grimshaw, R. (2012) *Housing and reintegration support for ex-prisoners with a conviction for a sexual offence*, London: Centre for Crime and Justice Studies.

Ministry of Justice (2008) *Third sector strategy: Improving policies and securing better public services through effective partnerships 2008-2011*, London: Ministry of Justice.

Ministry of Justice (2010) *Breaking the cycle: Effective punishment, rehabilitation and the sentencing of offenders*, London: The Stationery Office.

Ministry of Justice (2011a) *Competition strategy for offender services*, London: Ministry of Justice. Ministry of Justice (2011b) *Payment by Results – Work Programme pilots* (www.justice.gov.uk/offenders/payment-by-results/work-prog-pilots).

Ministry of Justice (2012a) *Offender Management Statistics (Quarterly) April – June 2012*, London: Ministry of Justice.

Ministry of Justice (2012b) *Proven reoffending, Quarterly*, London: Ministry of Justice.

Ministry of Justice (2012c) *Punishment and reform: Effective Probation Service*, London: Ministry of Justice.

Ministry of Justice (2012d) *Population Bulletin Weekly, 14 December* (www.justice.gov.uk/statistics/prisons-and-probation/prison-population-figures).

Moffitt, T., Casp, A., Rutter, M. and Silva, P. (2001) *Sex differences in antisocial behaviour: Conduct disorder, delinquency, and violence in the Dunedin Longitudinal Study*, Cambridge: Cambridge University Press.

Monaghan, M. (2012) 'The recent evolution of UK drug strategies: from maintenance to behaviour change?', *People, Place and Policy Online*, 6(1) (http://extra.shu.ac.uk/ppp-online/issue_1_300312/article_4.html).

Monaghan, M. and Wincup, E. (forthcoming) 'Work and the journey to recovery: exploring the implications of welfare reform for methadone maintenance clients', *International Journal of Drug Policy*.

Monbiot, G. (2012) 'We need to know who funds these thinktank lobbyists', *The Guardian*, 20 February (www.guardian.co.uk/commentisfree/2012/feb/20/who-funds-thinktank-lobbyists).

Moore, R. (2012) 'Beyond the prison walls: Some thoughts on prisoner "resettlement" in England and Wales', *Criminology and Criminal Justice*, 12(2): 129-47.

Morgan, R. (2006) 'With respect to order, the rules of the game have changed: New Labour's dominance of the "law and order" agenda', in T. Newburn and P. Rock (eds.) *The politics of crime control: Essays in honour of David Downes*, Oxford: Oxford University Press

Morgan, R. (2008) *Summary justice: Fast but fair?*, London: Centre for Crime and Justice Studies.

Morgan, R. (2011) 'Austerity, subsidiarity and parsimony: offending behaviour and criminalisation', in A. Silvestri (ed) *Lessons for the Coalition: An end of term report on New Labour and criminal justice*, London: Centre for Crime and Justice Studies.

Morgan, R. (2012) 'Crime and justice in the "Big Society"', *Criminology and Criminal Justice*, 12(5): 463-81.

Morgan, R. and Hough, M. (2007) 'The politics of criminological research' in R. King and E. Wincup (eds.) Doing Research on Crime and Justice, Oxford: Oxford University Press.

Morris, N. (2008) 'More than 3,600 new offences under Labour', *The Independent*, 4 September.

Morrison, W. (2009) 'What is crime? Contrasting definitions and perspectives', in C. Hale, K. Hayward, A. Wahidin and E. Wincup (eds) *Criminology* (2nd edn), Oxford: Oxford University Press.

Moss, K. and Stephens, M. (2005) *Crime reduction and the law*, London: Routledge.

Mulgan, G., Reeder, N., Aylott, M. and Bo'sher, L. (2011) *Social Impact investment: The challenge and opportunity of Social Impact Bonds*, London: The Young Foundation.

Mullholland, H. (2011) 'Duncan Smith blames riots on family breakdown and benefits system. Work and Pensions secretary's conference speech highlights "growing underclass" dependent on welfare', *The Guardian*, 3 October (www.guardian.co.uk/politics/2011/oct/03/duncan-smith-riots-benefits-system).

Muncie, J. (2001a) 'The construction and deconstruction of crime', in J. Muncie and E. McLaughlin (eds) *The problem of crime* (2nd edn), London: Sage Publications.

Muncie, J. (2001b) 'Prison histories: reform, repression and rehabilitation', in E. McLaughlin and J. Muncie (eds) *Controlling crime* (2nd edn), London: Sage Publications.

Munday, R. (1981) 'The Royal Commission on Criminal Procedure', *The Cambridge Law Journal*, 40(2): 193–8.

Murray, C. (1990) *The emerging British underclass*, London: Institute of Economic Affairs.

NatCen (National Centre for Social Research) (2009) *Anti-social behaviour Family Intervention Projects: Monitoring and evaluation*, London: Department for Children, Schools and Families.

NatCen (2011) *Monitoring and evaluation of Family Intervention Service and Projects between February 2007 and March 2011*, London: Department for Education.

National Audit Office (2010) *Tackling problem drug use*, London: National Audit Office.

National Treatment Agency for Substance Misuse (2012a) *Facts and figures* (www.ntas.nhs.uk/facts.aspx).

National Treatment Agency for Substance Misuse (2012b) *From access to recovery: Analysing six years of treatment data*, London: National Treatment Agency for Substance Misuse.

Naughton, M. (2005) 'Evidence-based policy and the government of the criminal justice system – only if the evidence fits!', *Critical Social Policy*, 25(1): 47-69.

Neale, J. (2006) 'Social exclusion, drugs and policy', in R. Hughes, R. Lart and P. Higate (eds) *Drugs: Policy and politics*, London: Longman.

Nellis, M. (2004) 'The tracking controversy: the roots of mentoring and electronic monitoring', *Youth Justice*, 4(2): 77-99.

Nellis, M. and Mair, G. (2012) 'England and Wales', in M. Nellis, K. Beyens and D. Kaminski (eds) *Electronically monitored punishment: International and critical perspectives*, London: Routledge.

NESS (National Evaluation of Sure Start) Team (2012) *The impact of Sure Start local programmes on seven year olds and their families*, London: Department for Education.

Newburn, T. (1999) 'Drug prevention and youth justice: issues of philosophy, practice and policy', *British Journal of Criminology*, 39(4): 609-24.

Newburn, T. (2002) 'Atlantic crossings: policy transfer and crime control in America and Britain', *Punishment and Society*, 4(2): 165-94.

Niven, S. and Stewart, D. (2005) *Resettlement outcomes on release from prison 2003*, Findings 178, London: Home Office.

Nutt, D. (2009) *Estimating drug harms: A risky business?*, London: Centre for Crime and Justice Studies.

O'Malley, P. (2004) *Risk, uncertainty and government*, London: Glasshouse Press.

O'Malley, P. (2006) 'Governmentality', in E. McLaughlin and J. Muncie (eds) *The SAGE dictionary of criminology* (2nd edn), London: Sage Publications.

ONS (Office for National Statistics) (2011) *General Lifestyle Survey, 2009 report*, London: ONS.

ONS (2012) *Crime in England and Wales, Quarterly first release to December 2011*, London: ONS.

Padfield, N. and Maruna, S. (2006) 'The revolving door: exploring the rise in recalls to prison', *Criminology and Criminal Justice*, 6(3): 329-52.

Pantazis, C. (2000) 'Fear of crime, vulnerability and poverty: evidence from the British Crime Survey', *British Journal of Criminology*, 40(3): 414-36.

Pantazis, C. (2006) 'Crime, "disorder", insecurity and social exclusion', in D. Gordon, R. Levitas and C. Pantazis (eds) *Poverty and social exclusion in Britain: The Millennium Survey*, Bristol: The Policy Press.

Parfrement-Hopkins, J. and Green, B. (2010) 'Public perceptions', in J. Flatley, C. Kershaw, K. Smith, R. Chaplin and D. Moon (eds) *Crime in England and Wales 2009/10: Findings from the British Crime Survey and police recorded crime* (3rd edn), Home Office Statistical Bulletin 12/10, London: Home Office.

Parrott, L. (2005) 'The political drivers of working in partnership', in R. Carnwell and J. Buchanan (eds) *Effective practice in health and social care: A partnership approach*, Buckingham: Open University Press.

Patrick, R. (2011) 'Work as the primary "duty" of the responsible citizen: a critique of this work-centric approach', *People, Place & Policy Online*, 6(1) (http://extra.shu.ac.uk/ppp-online/issue_1_300312/).

Pawson, R. (2002) 'Evidence-based policy: the promise of "realist synthesis"', *Evaluation*, 8(3): 340-58.

Payne, L. (2003) 'Anti-social behaviour', *Children and Society*, 17(4): 321-24.

Pearson, G. (1983) *Hooligan: A history of respectable fears*, Basingstoke: Macmillan.

Petersilia, J. (2003) *When prisoners come home: Parole and prisoner reentry*, New York: Cambridge University Press.

Philip, K. and Spratt, J. (2007) *A synthesis of published research on mentoring and befriending*, London: Mentoring and Befriending Foundation.

Police Foundation (2000) *Drugs and the law: Report of the Independent Inquiry into the Misuse of Drugs Act 1971*, London: Police Foundation.

Porteous, D. (2006) 'The rise and fall of mentoring in youth justice', *Prison Service Journal*, 170: 20-4.

President of the Council (1998) *Tackling drugs to build a better Britain: The government's ten year strategy for tackling drug misuse*, London: The Stationery Office.

Presdee, M. (2009) '"Volume crime" and everyday life', in C. Hale, K. Hayward, A. Wahidin and E. Wincup (eds) *Criminology* (2nd edn), Oxford: Oxford University Press.

Prison Reform Trust (2013) 'Privatisation will not rehabilitate our prisons', 21 February.

Raine, J. and Willson, M. (1993) *Managing criminal justice*, London: Harvester Wheatsheaf.

Raine, J. and Willson, M. (1995) 'New public management and criminal justice: how well does the coat fit?', *Public Management*, 15(1): 47-54.

Raine, J. and Willson, M. (1997) 'Beyond managerialism in criminal justice', *Howard Journal of Criminal Justice*, 36(1): 80-95.

Raynor, P. (2007) 'Theoretical perspectives on resettlement: what it is and how it might work', in A. Hucklesby and L. Hagley-Dickinson (eds) *Prisoner resettlement: Policy and practice*, Cullompton: Willan Publishing.

Raynor, P. and Robinson, G. (2009) *Rehabilitation, crime and justice* (2nd edn), Basingstoke: Palgrave Macmillan.

Respect Task Force (2006) *Respect Action Plan*, London: Respect Task Force.

Riots Communities and Victims Panel (2012) *After the riots: The final report of the Riots Communities and Victims Panel*, London: Riots Communities and Victims Panel.

Roberts, J. and Hough, M. (2005) *Understanding public attitudes to criminal justice*, Buckingham: Open University Press.

Rodger, J. (2008a) 'The criminalising of social policy', *Criminal Justice Matters*, 74: 18–19.

Rodger, J. (2008b) *Criminalising social policy: Anti-social behaviour and welfare in a de-civilised society*, Cullompton: Willan Publishing.

Rodger, J. (2012) 'Rehabilitation revolution in a Big Society', in A. Silvestri (ed) *Critical reflections: Social and criminal justice in the first year of the Coalition government*, London: Centre for Criminal Justice Studies.

Rolfe, H. (2001) *Barriers to employment for offenders and ex-offenders – Part two: A review of the literature*, Research Report No 155, London: Department for Work and Pensions (http://research.dwp.gov.uk/asd/asd5/report_abstracts/rr_abstracts/rra_155.asp).

Rough Sleepers Unit (1999) *Coming in from the cold: The government's strategy on rough sleeping*, London: Office of the Deputy Prime Minister.

Rowe, M. (2012) *Race and crime*, London: Sage Publications.

Royal Commission on Criminal Justice (1993) *Report of the Royal Commission on Criminal Justice*, Cm 2263, London: HMSO.

Royal Society for the Encouragement of Arts, Manufactures and Commerce (2007) *Drugs: Facing facts*, London: Royal Society for the Encouragement of Arts, Manufactures and Commerce.

Ruggerio, V. (1999) 'Drugs as a password and the law as a drug: discussing the legalisation of illicit substances', in N. South (ed) *Drugs: Cultures, controls and everyday life*, London: Sage Publications.

Russell, M. and Sciara, M. (2007) 'Why does the Government get defeated in the House of Lords? The Lords, the party system and British politics', *British Politics* 2(3): 299–322.

Ryan, M. (2003) *Penal policy and political culture in England and Wales*, Winchester: Waterside Press.

Sanders, A. (2011) 'What was New Labour thinking? New Labour's approach to criminal justice', in A. Silvestri (ed) *Lessons for the Coalition: An end of term report on New Labour and criminal justice* (www.crimeandjustice.org.uk/opus1830/end_of_term_report.pdf).

Sanders, A., Young, R. and Burton, M. (2010) Criminal justice, 4th edn, Oxford Oxford University Press.

Saraga, E. (2001) 'Dangerous places: the family as a site of crime', in J. Muncie and E. McLaughlin (eds) *The problem of crime* (2nd edn), London: Sage Publications.

Scottish Prisons Commission, The (2008) *Scotland's Choice Report of The Scottish Prisons Commission, July 2008*, Edinburgh: The Scottish Prisons Commission.

Scourfield, J. and Drakeford, M. (2002) 'New Labour and the "problem of men"', *Critical Social Policy*, 22(4): 619–40.

Seddon, T. (2007) 'Coerced treatment in the criminal justice system; conceptual, ethical and criminological issues', *Criminology and Criminal Justice*, 7(3): 269–86.

Senior, P., Crowther-Dowey, C. and Long, M. (2007) *Understanding the modernisation of criminal justice*, Buckingham: Open University Press.

Senior, P., Wong, K., Culshaw, A., Ellingworth, D. and O'Keefe, E. (2011) *Process evaluation of five Integrated Offender Management pioneer areas*, Ministry of Justice Research Series 4/11, London: Ministry of Justice.

Sevdiren, O. (2011) *Alternatives to imprisonment in England and Wales, Germany and Turkey: A comparative study*, New York: Springer Publishing.

Sharpe, J. (2001) 'Crime, order and historical change', in J. Muncie and E. McLaughlin (eds) *The problem of crime* (2nd edn), London: Sage Publications.

Shaw, S. (1982) *The people's justice: A major poll on public attitudes on crime and punishment*, London: Prison Reform Trust.

Shiner, M. (2006) 'Drugs, law and the regulation of harm', in R. Hughes, R. Lart and P. Higate (eds) *Drugs: Policy and politics*, London: Longman.

Shore, H. (2009) 'History of crime', in C. Hale, K. Hayward, A. Wahidin and E. Wincup (eds) *Criminology* (2nd edn), Oxford: Oxford University Press.

Silvestri, A. (2009) *Partners or prisoners: Voluntary sector independence in the world of commissioning and contestability*, London: Centre for Crime and Justice Studies.

Silvestri, A. (2011) *Lessons for the Coalition: An end of term report on New Labour and criminal justice*, London: Centre for Crime and Justice Studies.

Simon, J. (2007) *Governing through crime: How the war on crime transformed American democracy and created a culture of fear*, New York: Oxford University Press.

Skodbo, S., Brown, G., Deacon, S., Cooper, A., Hall, A., Millar, T., Smith, J. and Whitham, K. (2007) *The Drug Interventions Programme (DIP): Addressing drug use and offending through 'Tough Choices'*, Research Report 2, London: Home Office.

Slack, J. (2010) 'Labour is dreaming up 33 new crimes a month ... including barring you from swimming into the Titanic', *The Daily Mail*, 22 January.

Smith, R. (2007) *Youth justice: Ideas, policy, practice* (2nd edn), Cullompton: Willan Publishing.

Social Exclusion Unit (1998) *Rough sleeping: Report by the Social Exclusion Unit*, London: Cabinet Office.

Social Exclusion Unit (2002) *Reducing re-offending by ex-prisoners*, London: Cabinet Office.

Social Exclusion Task Force (2006) *Reaching out: An action plan on social exclusion*, London: Social Exclusion Task Force/Cabinet Office.

Social Exclusion Task Force (2007) *Reaching out: Think family. Analysis and themes from the Families at Risk review*, London: Social Exclusion Task Force/Cabinet Office.

Solesbury, W. (2001) *Evidence-based policy: Whence it came and where it is going*, ESRC Centre for Evidence-based Policy and Practice Working Paper 1 (www.kcl.ac.uk/sspp/departments/politicaleconomy/research/cep/pubs/papers/paper-01.aspx).

Solomon, E., Garside, R., Eades, C. and Rutherford M. (2007) *Ten years of criminal justice under Labour: An independent audit*, London: Centre for Crime and Justice Studies (www.crimeandjustice.org.uk/opus583.html).

Souhami, A. (2007) *Transforming youth justice: Occupational identity and cultural change*, Cullompton: Willan Publishing.

Sparks, R. (2001) 'Prisons, punishment and penality', in E. McLaughlin and J. Muncie (eds) *Controlling crime* (2nd edn), London: Sage Publications.

Squires, P. (ed) (2006) *Community safety: Critical perspectives on policy and practice*, Bristol: The Policy Press.

Stevens, A. (2010) 'Treatment services for drug users: contexts, mechanisms and outcomes', in. A. Hucklesby and E. Wincup (eds) *Drug interverntions in criminal justice*, Buckingham: Open University Press.

Stevens, A. (2011) *Drugs, crime and public health: The political economy of drug policy*, London: Routledge.

St Giles Trust (2012) *The ONE Service* (www.stgilestrust.org.uk/s/what-we-do/p486/the-one-service.html).

Stationery Office (1999) *Modernising Parliament: Reforming the House of Lords*, London: The Stationery Office.

Stone, D. (2001) 'Think tank, global lesson-drawing and networking social policy ideas', *Global Social Policy*, 1(3): 338-60.

Stone, N. (2003) 'Legal commentary: "Parenting Orders", "warnings and reprimands" and "age at time of offence" – human rights considerations', *Youth Justice*, 3(2): 112-22.

Sunstein, S. (2005) *Laws of fear: Beyond the precautionary principle*, Cambridge: Cambridge University Press.

Tempest, M. (2006) 'Blair launches "respect" action plan', *The Guardian*, 10 January (www.guardian.co.uk/politics/2006/jan/10/immigrationpolicy.ukcrime).

Travis, A. and Hirsch, A. (2010) 'Kenneth Clarke pledges to cut daily prison population', *The Guardian*, 20 October (www.guardian.co.uk/politics/2010/oct/20/kenneth-clarke-pledges-cut-prison-population).

Tremblay, R.E. and Craig, W.M (1995) 'Developmental crime prevention', in M. Tonry and D.P. Farrington (eds) *Building a safer society: Strategic approaches to crime prevention*, Chicago, IL: University of Chicago Press.

Turn2us (2012) *Benefits stigma in Britain*, London: Turn2us.

Turnbull, P. and Skinns, L. (2010) 'Drug Interventions Programme: neither success nor failure?', in A. Hucklesby and E. Wincup (eds) *Drug interventions in criminal justice*, Buckingham: Open University Press.

Turvill, W. (2012) 'ABCs: three national dailies increase circulation in September', *Press Gazette*, 12 October (www.pressgazette.co.uk/abcs-three-national-dailies-increase-circulation-september).

Uglow, S. (2009) 'The criminal justice system', in C. Hale, K. Hayward. A. Wahidin and E. Wincup (eds) *Criminology*, 2nd edn. Oxford: Oxford University Press.

UK Drug Policy Commission (2012) *A fresh approach to drugs: The final report of the UK Drug Policy Commission*, London: UK Drug Policy Commission.

UK Statistics Authority (2012) *Terms of reference of the Crime Statistics Advisory Committee (E&W) (2012)*, London: UK Statistics Authority.

van de Walle, S. (2009) 'Confidence in the criminal justice system': does experience count?', *British Journal of Criminology*, 49(3): 384-98.

Wacquant, L. (2009) *Punishing the poor: The neoliberal government of social insecurity*, Durham, NC: Duke University Press.

Walklate, S. (2011) 'Can the Big Society listen to gendered voices?', *Criminology and Criminal Justice*, 12(5): 495-9.

Warburton, H., Turnbull, P. and Hough, M. (2005) *Occasional and controlled heroin use: Not a problem?*, York: Joseph Rowntree Foundation.

Wardhaugh, J. (1991) 'Criminalising truancy', in T. Booth (ed) *Juvenile justice in the new Europe*, Sheffield: Joint Unit for Social Services Research.

Welsh Assembly Government (2011) *Programme for government 2011–2016* (wales.gov.uk/about/programmeforgov/;jsessionid=3D35E87148CCFD C7749BA6046D68BF67?lang=en).

West, D. and Woelke, P. (1997) 'England', in D. West and R. Green (eds) *Sociolegal control of homosexuality: A multi-nation comparison*, New York: Springer Publishing.

Whitfield, D. (2012) 'The Payment-by-Results road to marketisation', in A. Silvestri (ed) *Critical reflections: Social and criminal justice in the first year of the Coalition government*, London: Centre for Criminal Justice Studies.

Wiener, M. (1990) *Reconstructing the criminal law: Culture, law and policy in England, 1830–1914*, Cambridge: Cambridge University Press.

Williams, Z. (2012) 'The real "problem" with these families is that they're poor', *The Guardian*, 18 May.

Wilson, G. (2011 'Boris Johnson tells Ken Clarke: no soft justice', *The Sun*, 8 March.

Wincup, E. (2002) *Residential work with offenders: Reflexive accounts of practice*, Aldershot: Ashgate.

Wincup, E. (2011a) 'Drugs, drug abuse, and drug policy', in G. Ritzer and J. Ryan (eds) *The concise encyclopaedia of sociology*, Malden, MA: Wiley-Blackwell.

Wincup, E. (2011b) 'Carrots and sticks: problem drug users and welfare reform', *Criminal Justice Matters*, 84: 22-3.

Wincup, E. and Hucklesby, A. (2007) 'Researching and evaluating resettlement', in A. Hucklesby and L. Hagley-Dickinson (eds) *Prisoner resettlement: Policy and practice*, Cullompton: Willan Publishing.

Wincup, E. and Traynor, P. (2013) 'Drugs, alcohol and crime', in C. Hale, K. Hayward, A. Wahidin and E. Wincup (eds) *Criminology*, Oxford: Oxford University Press.

Wincup, E., Buckland, G. and Baylis, R. (2003) *Youth homelessness and substance use: A report to the Drugs and Alcohol Research Unit*, Home Office Research Study 258, London: Home Office.

Winlow, S. and Hall, S. (2006) *Violent night: Urban leisure and contemporary culture*, Oxford: Berg.

Wintour, P. (2012) 'Iain Duncan Smith to unveil new ways of measuring child poverty. Work and Pensions secretary will downgrade Labour's method of comparing family incomes in favour of other indicators', *The Guardian*, 14 November (www.guardian.co.uk/society/2012/nov/14/iain-duncan-smith-child-poverty).

Wood, J. and Viki, G. (2004) 'Public attitudes towards crime and punishment', in J. Adler (ed) *Forensic psychology: Debates, concepts and practice*, Cullompton: Willan Publishing.

Worrall, A. and Canton, R. (2013) 'Community sentences and offender management for adults', in C. Hale, K. Hayward, A. Wahidin and E. Wincup (eds) *Criminology* (3rd edn), Oxford: Oxford University Press.

Worrall, A. and Hoy, C. (2005) *Punishment in the community: Managing offenders, making choices*, Cullompton: Willan Publishing.

Young, J. (1999) *The exclusive society: Social exclusion, crime and difference in late modernity*, London: Sage Publications.

Young, K., Ashby, D., Boaz, A. and Grayson, L. (2002) 'Social science and the evidence-based policy movement', *Social Policy and Society*, 1(3): 215-22.

Young, R. and Sanders, A. (1994) 'Royal Commission on Criminal Justice: A confidence trick?', *Oxford Journal of Legal Studies*, 14: 435-48.

Youth Justice Board (2005) *Risk and protective factors*, London: Youth Justice Board.

Zedner, L. (2004) *Criminal justice*, Oxford: Oxford University Press.

Index